MANUAL
ON HUMAN RIGHTS
AND THE ENVIRONMENT

French edition: *Manuel sur les droits de l'homme et l'environnement*

ISBN 978-92-871-7318-8

Cover illustration: 2012, Documents and Publications Production Department, Council of Europe

Illustrations: Alfonso de Salas

Council of Europe Publishing
F-67075 Strasbourg Cedex
http://book.coe.int

ISBN 978-92-871-7319-5

© Council of Europe, 2006, 2012
First edition, 2006
Second edition, 2012
Printed at the Council of Europe

Contents

ABBREVIATIONS

CDDH	Steering Committee for Human Rights
CIS	Commonwealth of Independent States
CITIES	Convention on International Trade in Endangered Species of Wild Fauna and Flora
DH-DEV	Committee of Experts for the Development of Human Rights
ECJ	European Court of Justice
ECS	Environmental Cross-cutting Strategy
ECSR	European Committee for Social Rights
EEA	European Environment Agency
EEL	European Environmental Law
EIA	Environmental Impact Assessment
ETS	European Treaty Series
EU	European Union
FAO	Food and Agricultural Organization
GC	Grand Chamber
HUDOC	Human Rights Documentation (Online Database)
ICJ	International Court of Justice
IEEP	Institute for European Environmental Policy
IPPC	International Plant Protection Convention
ITLOS	International Tribunal for the Law of the Sea
IUCN	International Union for Conservation of Nature
NGO	Non-Governmental Organisation
PACE	Parliamentary Assembly of the Council of Europe
UNCED	United Nations Conference on Environment and Development
UNECE	United Nations Economic Commission for Europe
UNEP	United Nations Environment Programme
UNESCO	United Nations Educational, Scientific and Cultural Organization
UNFCCC	United Nations Framework Convention on Climate Change
WTO	World Trade Organization

PRELIMINARY REMARKS

WHAT IS THE AIM OF THIS MANUAL?

The main aim of this manual is to increase the understanding of the relationship between the protection of human rights under the European Convention on Human Rights ("the Convention") and the environment and thereby to contribute to strengthening environmental protection at the national level. To achieve this aim, the manual seeks to provide information about the case-law of the European Court of Human Rights ("the Court") in this field. In addition, it will highlight the impact of the European Social Charter and relevant interpretations of the European Social Charter ("the Charter") by the European Committee of Social Rights ("the Committee").

WHO IS THE TARGET AUDIENCE OF THIS MANUAL?

The manual is intended to be of practical use for public authorities (be they national, regional or local), decision-makers, legal professionals and the general public.

IS THE ENVIRONMENT PROTECTED UNDER INTERNATIONAL LAW?

The environment is protected by international law despite the absence of a general framework convention. Multifarious international treaties govern specific environmental issues, like climate change or biodiversity. Because of these treaties and customary international law various legal obligations to protect the environment are placed upon states, e.g. duties to inform, co-operate or limit emissions.

IS THE ENVIRONMENT PROTECTED UNDER THE EUROPEAN CONVENTION ON HUMAN RIGHTS AND THE EUROPEAN SOCIAL CHARTER?

Neither the Convention nor the Charter are designed to provide a general protection of the environment as such and do not expressly guarantee a right to a sound, quiet and healthy environment. However, the Convention and the Charter indirectly offer a certain degree of protection with regard to environmental matters, as demonstrated by the evolving case-law of the Court and decisions of the Committee on Social Rights in this area.

The Court has increasingly examined complaints in which individuals have argued that a breach of one of their Convention rights has resulted from adverse environmental factors. Environmental factors may affect individual Convention rights in three different ways:

- First, the human rights protected by the Convention may be directly affected by adverse environmental factors. For instance, toxic smells from a factory or rubbish tip might have a negative impact on the health of individuals. Public authorities may be obliged to take measures to ensure that human rights are not seriously affected by adverse environmental factors.

- Second, adverse environmental factors may give rise to certain procedural rights for the individual concerned. The Court has established that public authorities must observe certain requirements as regards information and communication, as well as participation in decision-making processes and access to justice in environmental cases.

- Third, the protection of the environment may also be a legitimate aim justifying interference with certain individual human rights. For example, the Court has established that the right to peaceful enjoyment of one's possessions may be restricted if this is considered necessary for the protection of the environment.

WHICH RIGHTS OF THE CONVENTION AND THE SOCIAL CHARTER CAN BE AFFECTED BY ENVIRONMENTAL FACTORS?

The Court has already identified in its case-law issues related to the environment which could affect the right to life (Article 2), the right to respect for private and family life as well as the home (Article 8), the right to a fair trial and to have access to a court (Article 6), the right to receive and impart information and ideas (Article 10), the right to an effective remedy (Article 13) and the right to the peaceful enjoyment of one's possessions (Article 1 of Protocol No. 1).

The issue of passive smoking has been raised in connection with the right to prohibition of inhuman or degrading treatment (Article 3 of the Convention)[1] but at present there is not sufficient case-law to be able to draw up any clear principles on environmental protection at the European level.

---

1. *Florea v. Romania*, judgment of 14 September 2010. In two earlier previous cases on passive smoking the applicants had not alleged a violation of Article 3 in view of inhuman or degrading treatment, but had referred to Article 2 (right to life) and Article 8 (right to respect for family life). See *Aparicio Benito v. Spain* (No. 2), decision of 13 November 2006 and *Stoine Hristov v. Bulgaria* judgment of 16 January 2009.

Likewise, the Committee has interpreted the right to protection of health (Article 11) under the European Social Charter as including the right to a healthy environment.

INTRODUCTION

The environment and environmental protection have only recently become a concern of the international community. After World War Two, the reconstruction of the economy and lasting peace were the first priorities; this included the guarantee of civil and political as well as social and economic human rights. However, in the subsequent half century the environment has become a prominent concern, which has also had an impact on international law. Although the main human rights instruments (the 1948 Universal Declaration of Human Rights, the 1950 European Convention on Human Rights, the 1961 European Social Charter, the 1966 International Covenants), all drafted well before full awareness of environmental issues arose, do not refer to the environment, today it is commonly accepted that human rights and the environment are interrelated.[2]

As recently as 1972, the first UN Conference on the Human Environment, which took place in Stockholm, shed light on the relationship between respect for human rights and the protection of the environment. Indeed, the preamble to the Stockholm Declaration proclaims that "both aspects of man's environment, the natural and manmade, are essential to his well-being and to the enjoyment of basic human rights – even the right to life itself". Further on, Principle I of the Stockholm Declaration stressed that "Man has the fundamental right to freedom, equality and adequate conditions of life, in an environment of a quality that permits a life of dignity and well-being, and he bears a solemn responsibility to protect and improve the environment for present and future generations".

The 1992 Rio de Janeiro Conference on Environment and Development (UNCED) focused on the link that exists between human rights and the environment in terms of procedural rights. Principle 10 of the Declaration adopted during the Rio Conference provides that:

Environmental issues are best handled with participation of all concerned citizens, at the relevant level. At the national level, each individual shall have appropriate access to information concerning the environment that is held by public authorities, including information on hazardous materials and activities in their communities, and the opportunity to participate in decision-making processes. States shall facilitate and encourage public awareness and participation by making information widely available. Effective access to

---

2.   Even to the point that it is suggested that environmental rights belong to a "third generation of human rights". See Karel Vasak, "Human Rights: A Thirty-Year Struggle: the Sustained Efforts to give Force of law to the Universal Declaration of Human Rights", *UNESCO Courier* 30:11, Paris: United Nations Educational, Scientific, and Cultural Organization, November 1977.

judicial and administrative proceedings, including redress and remedy, shall be provided.

Work has continued ever since on the issue of human rights and the environment in the framework of the UN. In this regard the final report on "Human rights and the environment" of Special Rapporteur Ms F.Z. Ksentini is notable. It contains a "draft declaration of principles on human rights and the environment[3] another milestone is the Johannesburg Summit of 2002, which recalls and refines the principles of the Rio Declaration of 1992.

Currently, no comprehensive legally binding instrument for the protection of the environment exists globally. Meanwhile, various specific legally binding instruments and political documents have been adopted at the international and European levels to ensure environmental protection. For example, at the European level the right to a healthy environment has been recognised for the first time in the operative provisions of the Convention on Access to Information, Public Participation in Decision-Making and Access to Justice in Environmental Matters (Aarhus Convention). However, the scope of the Aarhus Convention is the guarantee of procedural rights, but not the right to a healthy environment as such. The substantial right is presumed to exist by the Convention. Recently, the Almaty Guidelines and the Protocol on Pollutant Release and Transfer Registers have enhanced protection of the Convention.[4]

Furthermore, human rights treaties such as the European Convention for the Protection of Human Rights and Fundamental Freedoms and the European Social Charter have been interpreted as including obligations pertaining to the protection of the environment, despite the fact that none contain a

---

3. Human Rights and the Environment, Final Report, Ms F.Z. Ksentini, Special Rapporteur, UN Doc.E/CN.4/Sub.2/1994/9.
4. The Convention on Access to Information, Public Participation in Decision-Making and Access to Justice in Environmental Matters (adopted in Aarhus, Denmark, on 25 June 1998) was elaborated within the United Nations Economic Commission for Europe (UN/ECE). It has been ratified to date (31 December 2010) by 42 of the Council of Europe member States as well as Belarus. The European Union has also ratified it. The Aarhus Convention entered into force in 2001. For more information: www.unece.org/env

    Almaty Guidelines on promoting the application of the principles of the Aarhus Convention in International Forums, Annexed to Report of the Second Meeting of Parties, UN Doc. ECE/MP.PP/2005/2/Add.5 of 20 June 2005, available at: www.unece.org/env/documents/2005/pp/ece/ece.mp.pp.2005.2.add.5.e.pdf

    Protocol on Pollutant Release and Transfer Registers to the Convention on Access to Information, Public Participation in Decision-Making and Access to Justice in Environmental Matters, signed 21 May 2003, entry into force 8 October 2009. Currently, 26 Council of Europe member states have become parties to it.

right to the environment explicitly. However, a number of cases raising environmental issues have come before the Court who consequently pronounced on them. It referred to rights included in the 1950 Convention on which issues, such as noise levels from airports, industrial pollution, or town planning, undeniably had an impact.

Conscious of these developments, the Committee of Ministers of the Council of Europe decided in 2004, following a recommendation of the Parliamentary Assembly,[5] that it is an appropriate time to raise awareness of the Court's case-law, which has led to the drafting of the first version of this manual.[6] Subsequently in 2009, the Committee of Ministers decided again,[7] upon the recommendation of the Parliamentary Assembly,[8] to update the manual in the light of the relevant new case-law. Moreover, when approving the first version of the manual, the Steering Committee for Human Rights (CDDH) had already decided that subsequent versions should also reflect the relevant standards set out by other international organisations and the Council of Europe bodies, notably the European Committee of Social Rights (ECSR).[9] Therefore, the present version of the manual has been extended to include references to other environmental protection instruments, a collection of examples of national good practices and an environmental law bibliography, in addition to the updated sections on the case-law of the European Court of Human Rights.

The manual aims at assisting people – at the local, regional or national level – in solving problems they encounter in pursuit of a sound, quiet and healthy environment, thereby contributing to strengthening environmental protection at the national level. It strives primarily to describe the extent to which environmental protection is embedded in the European Convention on Human Rights and the European Social Charter. It will also refer to other international instruments with direct relevance for the interpretation of the Convention and Charter.

---

5. Recommendation (2003) 1614 of the Parliamentary Assembly, adopted on 27 June 2003.
6. Terms of reference to draft this manual were received by the Steering Committee for Human Rights (CDDH) – a body composed of governmental representatives from the 46 member States – from the Committee of Ministers in a decision of 21 January 2004 (869th meeting). The CDDH entrusted this task to a subordinate intergovernmental body of experts: the Committee of Experts for the Development of Human Rights (DH-DEV). Website: www.coe.int/cddh
7. Document CDDH(2009)019, paragraph 19.
8. Recommendation 1885 (2009) of the Parliamentary Assembly, adopted on 30 September 2009.
9. Document CDDH (2005) 016, paragraph 4.

The manual consists of two parts. The first part contains an executive summary of the principles which govern environmental protection based on human rights. Most of the principles are derived from the relevant case-law of the Court of Human Rights and a few from the relevant decisions and conclusions of the Committee of Social Rights. The second part recapitulates these principles explaining them in more detail. The explanations refer to concrete case-law, illustrating the context against which the principles have been considered. The cases referred to are not exhaustive, although the drafters have sought to select those that are most relevant. The second part is divided into two sections. Whereas section A will solely focus on the Court's case-law, section B will shed light on the European Social Charter and the decisions and conclusions of the European Committee on Social Rights. The principles explained in section A are divided into seven thematic chapters. For the purpose of clarity the first chapters deal with substantive rights (chapters I to III), while the following chapters cover procedural rights (chapters IV to VI). The last chapter of this section deals with the territorial scope of the Convention's application.

Efforts have been made to keep the language as simple and clear as possible, while at the same time remaining legally accurate and faithful to the Court's reasoning. In instances where technical language has proved unavoidable, the reader will find concise definitions in an appended glossary (Appendix I). A list of the most relevant judgments and decisions of the Court pertaining to environmental questions is also enclosed at the end of the manual (Appendix II). In addition, a second list containing European Court of Human Rights' judgments that refer explicitly to other international environmental protection instruments has been included (Appendix III). Moreover, some examples of good practices at the national level complement the substantial chapters of this manual. This list of national good practices provides some useful advice to policy-makers at national and local levels who wish to contribute to environmental protection. The examples often follow the principles derived from the Court's case-law as well as other standards at the European and international level (Appendix IV). Furthermore, as the manual cannot provide an in-depth analysis of each specific aspect of the Court's case-law and the Committee's decisions, especially, with regard to all international environmental instruments, whose proper understanding is indispensible for the interpretation of the Convention and the Charter, an updated web bibliography and a list of relevant readings has been included (Appendix V and VI). Lastly, an index has been added for quick reference (Appendix VII).

Importantly, nothing in this manual seeks to add or subtract to rights under the Convention and Charter as interpreted by the Court and the Committee. It is simply a guide to the existing case-law and decisions at the time of publication.[10]

Before considering the main part of the manual, some comments are necessary on the definition of "environment". In the absence of a universal framework convention no generally accepted legal definition exists at present. It appears, however, that most proposed definitions are rather anthropocentric. For instance, the International Court of Justice held in its Advisory Opinion on the Legality of the Threat or Use of Nuclear Weapons that "the environment is not an abstraction but represents the living space, the quality of life and the very health of human beings, including generations unborn".[11]

Among the environment related conventions elaborated within the framework of the Council of Europe,[12] only one endeavours to define the scope of the concept "environment". The following broad definition can be found in the Convention on Civil Liability for Damage Resulting from Activities Dangerous to the Environment (Lugano, 21 June 1993) which provides in its Article 2 (10):

"Environment" includes:

– natural resources both abiotic and biotic, such as air, water, soil, fauna and flora and the interaction between the same factors;

– property which forms part of the cultural heritage; and

– the characteristic aspects of the landscape.

At the time of the elaboration of the European Convention on Human Rights and the European Social Charter the environment was not a concern and therefore they do not contain a definition of the environment. However, the question of the precise definition of the environment is not of vital importance to understand the case-law of the Court and the decisions of the Committee. Neither the European Convention on Human Rights nor the European Social Charter protects the environment as such, but various

---

10. The principles contained in this revised manual are based on case-law and decisions until July 2011.
11. *Legality of the Threat or Use of Nuclear Weapons*, Advisory opinion of 8 July 1996, ICJ. Reports (1996) 226, paragraph 29.
12. Convention on Civil Liability for Damage resulting from Activities Dangerous to the Environment (ETS No 150); Convention on the Protection of Environment through Criminal Law (ETS No. 172); European Landscape Convention (ETS No. 176).

individual rights provided for in these treaties which might be affected by the environment. Hence, it is rather the impact on the individual than the environment that both the Court and the Committee are concerned with.

Part I: Executive summary

SECTION A – PRINCIPLES DERIVED FROM THE EUROPEAN CONVENTION ON HUMAN RIGHTS

CHAPTER I:
RIGHT TO LIFE AND THE ENVIRONMENT

(a) The right to life is protected under Article 2 of the Convention. This Article does not solely concern deaths resulting directly from the actions of the agents of a State, but also lays down a positive obligation on States to take appropriate steps to safeguard the lives of those within their jurisdiction. This means that public authorities have a duty to take steps to guarantee the rights of the Convention even when they are threatened by other (private) persons or activities that are not directly connected with the State.

(b) The Court has found that the positive obligation on States may apply in the context of dangerous activities, such as nuclear tests, the operation of chemical factories with toxic emissions or waste-collection sites, whether carried out by public authorities themselves or by private companies. In general, the extent of the obligations of public authorities depends on factors such as the harmfulness of the dangerous activities and the foreseeability of the risks to life.

(c) In addition, the Court requires States to discharge their positive obligation to prevent the loss of life also in cases of natural disasters, even though they are as such, beyond human control, in contrast to the case of dangerous activities where States are required to hold ready appropriate warning and defence mechanisms.

(d) In the first place, public authorities may be required to take measures to prevent infringements of the right to life as a result of dangerous activities or natural disasters. This entails, above all, the primary duty of a State to put in place a legislative and administrative framework which includes:

- making regulations which take into account the special features of a situation or an activity and the level of potential risk to life. In the case of dangerous activities this entails regulations that govern the licensing, setting-up, operation, security and supervision of such activities;

- placing particular emphasis on the public's right to information concerning such activities. In cases of natural disasters this includes the maintenance of an adequate defence and warning infrastructure;

- providing for appropriate procedures for identifying shortcomings in the technical processes concerned and errors committed by those responsible.

(e) Secondly, where loss of life may be the result of an infringement of the right to life, the relevant public authorities must provide an adequate response, judicial or otherwise. They must ensure that the legislative and administrative framework is properly implemented and that breaches of the right to life are repressed and punished as appropriate.

(f) This response by the State includes the duty to initiate promptly an independent and impartial investigation. The investigation must be capable of ascertaining the circumstances in which the incident took place and identifying shortcomings in the operation of the regulatory system. It must also be capable of identifying the public officials or authorities involved in the chain of events in issue.

(g) If the infringement of the right to life is not intentional, civil, administrative or even disciplinary remedies may be a sufficient response. However, the Court has found that, in particular in the case of dangerous activities, where the public authorities were fully aware of the likely consequences and disregarded the powers vested in them, hence failing to take measures that are necessary and sufficient to avert certain risks which might involve loss of life, Article 2 may require that those responsible for endangering life be charged with a criminal offence or prosecuted.

CHAPTER II:
RESPECT FOR PRIVATE AND FAMILY LIFE

(a) The right to respect for private and family life and the home are protected under Article 8 of the Convention. This right implies respect for the quality of private life as well as the enjoyment of the amenities of one's home ("living space").

(b) Environmental degradation does not necessarily involve a violation of Article 8 as it does not include an express right to environmental protection or nature conservation.

(c) For an issue to arise under Article 8, the environmental factors must directly and seriously affect private and family life or the home. Thus, there are two issues which the Court must consider – whether a causual link exists between the activity and the negative impact on the individual and whether the adverse have attained a certain threshold of harm. The assessment of that minimum threshold depends on all the circumstances of the case, such as the intensity and duration of the nuisance and its physical or mental effects, as well as on the general environmental context.

(d) While the objective of Article 8 is essentially that of protecting the individual against arbitrary interference by public authorities, it may also imply in some cases an obligation on public authorities to adopt positive measures designed to secure the rights enshrined in this article. This obligation does not only apply in cases where environmental harm is directly caused by State activities but also when it results from private sector activities. Public authorities must make sure that such measures are implemented so as to guarantee rights protected under Article 8. The Court has furthermore explicitly recognised that public authorities may have a duty to inform the public about environmental risks. Moreover, the Court has stated with regard to the scope of the positive obligation that it is generally irrelevant of whether a situation is assessed from the perspective of paragraph 1 of Article 8 which, *inter alia,* relates to the positive obligations of State authorities, or paragraph 2 asking whether a State interference was justified, as the principles applied are almost identical.

(e) Where decisions of public authorities affect the environment to the extent that there is an interference with the right to respect for private or family life or the home, they must accord with the conditions set out in Article 8 paragraph 2. Such decisions must thus be provided for by law and follow a legitimate aim, such as the economic well-being of the country or the protection of the rights and freedoms of others. In addition, they must be proportionate to the legitimate aim pursued: for this purpose, a fair balance must be struck between the interest of the individual and the interest of the community as a whole. Since the social and technical aspects of environmental issues are often difficult to assess, the relevant public authorities are best placed to determine what might be the best policy. Therefore they enjoy in principle a wide margin of appreciation in determining how the balance should be struck. The Court may nevertheless assess whether the public authorities have approached the problem with due diligence and have taken all the competing interests into consideration.

(f) In addition, the Court has recognised the preservation of the environment, in particular in the framework of planning policies, as a legitimate aim justifying certain restrictions by public authorities on a person's right to respect for private and family life and the home.

CHAPTER III:
PROTECTION OF PROPERTY

(a) Under Article 1 of Protocol No. 1 to the Convention, individuals are entitled to the peaceful enjoyment of their possessions, including protection from unlawful deprivation of property. This provision does not, in principle, guarantee the right to continue to enjoy those possessions in a pleasant environment. Article 1 of Protocol No. 1 also recognises that public authorities are entitled to control the use of property in accordance with the general interest. In this context the Court has found that the environment is an increasingly important consideration.

(b) The general interest in the protection of the environment can justify certain restrictions by public authorities on the individual right to the peaceful enjoyment of one's possessions. Such restrictions should be lawful and proportionate to the legitimate aim pursued. Public authorities enjoy a wide margin of appreciation in deciding with regard both to the choice of the means of enforcement and to the ascertaining whether the consequences of enforcement are justified in the general interest. However, the measures taken by public authorities must be proportionate and strike a fair balance between the interests involved, and here environmental preservation plays an increasingly important role.

(c) On the other hand, protection of the individual right to the peaceful enjoyment of one's possessions may require the public authorities to ensure certain environmental standards. The effective exercise of this right does not depend merely on the public authorities' duty not to interfere, but may require them to take positive measures to protect this right, particularly where there is a direct link between the measures an applicant may legitimately expect from the authorities and his or her effective enjoyment of his or her possessions. The Court has found that such an obligation may arise in respect of dangerous activities and to a lesser extent in situations of natural disasters.

CHAPTER IV:
INFORMATION AND COMMUNICATION

*Right to receive and impart information
and ideas on environmental matters*

(a) The right to receive and impart information and ideas is guaranteed by Article 10 of the Convention. In the particular context of the environment, the Court has found that there exists a strong public interest in enabling individuals and groups to contribute to the public debate by disseminating information and ideas on matters of general public interest.

(b) Restrictions by public authorities on the right to receive and impart information and ideas, including on environmental matters, must be prescribed by law and follow a legitimate aim. Measures interfering with this right must be proportionate to the legitimate aim pursued and a fair balance must therefore be struck between the interest of the individual and the interest of the community as a whole.

(c) Freedom to receive information under Article 10 can neither be construed as imposing on public authorities a general obligation to collect and disseminate information relating to the environment of their own motion.

Access to information on environmental matters

(a) However, Articles 2 and 8 of the Convention may impose a specific positive obligation on public authorities to ensure a right of access to information in relation to environmental issues in certain circumstances.

(b) This obligation to *ensure access to information* is generally complemented by the positive obligations of the public authorities to *provide information* to those persons whose right to life under Article 2 or whose right to respect for private and family life and the home under Article 8 are threatened. The Court has found that in the particular context of dangerous activities falling within the responsibility of the State, special emphasis should be placed on the public's right to information. Additionally, the Court held that States are duty-bound based on Article 2 to "adequately inform the public about any life threatening emergencies, including natural disasters."

(c) Access to information is of importance to individuals because it can allay their fears and enables them to assess the environmental danger to which they may be exposed.

(d) Moreover, the Court has established criteria on the construction of the procedures used to provide information. It held that when public authorities engage in dangerous activities which they know involve adverse risks to health, they must establish an effective and accessible procedure to enable individuals to seek all relevant and appropriate information. Moreover, if environmental and health impact assessments are carried out, the public needs to have access to those study results.

CHAPTER V:
DECISION-MAKING PROCESSES
IN ENVIRONMENTAL MATTERS
AND PUBLIC PARTICIPATION IN THEM

(a) When making decisions which relate to the environment, public authorities must take into account the interests of individuals who may be affected. In this context, it is important that the public is able to make representations to the public authorities.

(b) Where public authorities have complex issues of environmental and economic policy to determine, the decision-making process must involve appropriate investigations and studies in order to predict and evaluate in advance the effects on the environment and to enable them to strike a fair balance between the various conflicting interests at stake. The Court has stressed the importance of public access to the conclusions of such studies and to information which would enable individuals to assess the danger to which they are exposed. However, this does not mean that decisions can be taken only if comprehensive and measurable data are available in relation to each and every aspect of the matter to be decided.

CHAPTER VI:
ACCESS TO JUSTICE AND OTHER REMEDIES
IN ENVIRONMENTAL MATTERS

(a) Several provisions of the Convention guarantee that individuals should be able to commence judicial or administrative proceedings in order to protect their rights. Article 6 guarantees the right to a fair trial, which the Court has found includes the right of access to a court. Article 13 guarantees to persons, who have an arguable claim that their rights and freedoms as set forth in the Convention have been violated, an effective remedy before a national authority. Moreover, the Court has inferred procedural requirements from certain provisions of the Convention, such as Articles 2 and 8 and Article 1 of Protocol No. 1. All these provisions may apply in cases where human rights and environmental issues are involved.

(b) The right of access to a court under Article 6 will as a rule come into play when a "civil right or obligation", within the meaning of the Convention, is the subject of a "dispute". This includes the right to see final and enforceable court decisions executed and implies that all parties, including public authorities, must respect court decisions.

(c) The right of access to a court guaranteed by Article 6 applies if there is a sufficiently direct link between the environmental problem at issue and the civil right invoked; mere tenuous connections or remote consequences are not sufficient. In case of a serious, specific and imminent environmental risk, Article 6 may be invoked if the danger reaches a degree of probability which makes the outcome of the proceedings directly decisive for the rights of those individuals concerned.

(d) Environmental associations which are entitled to bring proceedings in the national legal system to defend the interests of their members may invoke the right of access to a court when they seek to defend the economic interests of their members (e.g. their personal assets and lifestyle). However, they will not necessarily enjoy a right of access to a court when they are only defending a broad public interest.

(e) Where public authorities have to determine complex questions of environmental and economic policy, they must ensure that the decision-making process takes account of the rights and interests of the individuals whose rights under Articles 2 and 8 may be affected. Where such individuals consider that their interests have not been given sufficient weight in the decision-making process, they should be able to appeal to a court.

(f) In addition to the right of access to a court as described above, Article 13 guarantees that persons, who have an arguable claim that their rights and freedoms as set forth in the Convention have been violated, must have an effective remedy before a national authority.

(g) The protection afforded by Article 13 does not go so far as to require any particular form of remedy. The State has a margin of appreciation in determining how it gives effect to its obligations under this provision. The nature of the right at stake has implications for the type of remedy which the state is required to provide. Where for instance violations of the rights enshrined in Article 2 are alleged, compensation for economic and non-economic loss should in principle be possible as part of the range of redress available. However, neither Article 13 nor any other provision of the Convention guarantees an individual a right to secure the prosecution and conviction of those responsible.

(h) Environmental protection concerns may in addition to Articles 6 and 13 impact the interpretation of other procedural articles, such as Article 5 which sets out the rules for detention and arrest of person. The Court has found that in the case of offences against the environment, like the massive spilling of oil by ships, a strong legal interest of the public exist to prosecute those responsible. The Court recognised that maritime environmental protection law has evolved constantly. Hence, it is in the light of those "new realities" that the Convention articles need to be interpreted. Consequently, environmental damage can be of a degree that justifies arrest and detention, as well as imposition of substantial amount of bail.

CHAPTER VII:
PRINCIPLES FROM THE COURT'S CASE-LAW:
TERRITORIAL SCOPE OF THE CONVENTION'S APPLICATION

(a) The Court has not decided on cases relating to environmental protection which raise extra-territorial and transboundary issues. The Court has produced, in different contexts, ample case-law elaborating the principles of the extra-territorial and transboundary application of the Convention. The principles that are potentially the most relevant for environmental issues are briefly explained. However, as they have been developed under very different factual circumstances, it will be up to the Court to determine if and how they can be applied to cases concerning the environment.

SECTION B – PRINCIPLES DERIVED
FROM THE EUROPEAN SOCIAL CHARTER
AND THE REVISED EUROPEAN SOCIAL CHARTER

CHAPTER I:
RIGHT TO PROTECTION OF HEALTH AND THE ENVIRONMENT

(a) Article 11 on the right to protection of health has been interpreted by the Committee as including the right to a healthy environment. The Committee has noted the complementarity between the right to health under Article 11 of the Charter and Articles 2 and 3 of the European Convention on Human Rights. As a consequence, several Committee conclusions on State reports regarding the right to health, specifically indicate that the measures required under Article 11, paragraph 1 should be designed to remove the causes of ill health resulting from environmental threats such as pollution.

(b) States are responsible for activities which are harmful to the environment whether they are carried out by the public authorities themselves or by a private company.

(c) Overcoming pollution is an objective that can only be achieved gradually. Nevertheless, States must strive to attain this objective within a reasonable time, by showing measurable progress and making best possible use of the resources at their disposal. The measures taken by States with a view to overcoming pollution are assessed with reference to their national legislation and undertakings entered into with regard to the European Union and the United Nations and in terms of how the relevant law is applied in practice.

(d) In order to combat air pollution States are required to implement an appropriate strategy which should include the following measures:

- develop and regularly update sufficiently comprehensive environmental legislation and regulations;
- take specific steps, such as modifying equipment, introducing threshold values for emissions and measuring air quality, to prevent air pollution at local level and to help to reduce it on a global scale;
- ensure that environmental standards and rules are properly applied, through appropriate supervisory machinery;
- inform and educate the public, including pupils and students at school, about both general and local environmental problems.

(e) In a State where a part of its energy source derives from nuclear power plants, this State is under the obligation to prevent related hazards for the communities living in the areas of risk. Moreover, all States are required to protect their population against the consequences of nuclear accidents taking place abroad and having an effect within their territory.

(f) Under Article 11 States must apply a policy which bans the use, production and sale of asbestos and products containing it.

Part II: Environmental protection principles

SECTION A – PRINCIPLES DERIVED FROM THE EUROPEAN CONVENTION ON HUMAN RIGHTS

The European Convention for the Protection of Human Rights and Fundamental Freedoms (ETS No. 5) ("the Convention") was signed in 1950 by the founding States of the Council of Europe. This international organisation is based in Strasbourg and currently has 47 member states.[13] All member states have ratified the Convention and therefore accept the jurisdiction of the Court which ensures compliance with the Convention.

The strength of the Convention is based on the fact that it sets up an effective control system in relation to the rights and freedoms which it guarantees to individuals. Anyone who considers himself or herself to be a victim of a violation of one of these rights may submit a complaint to the Court provided that certain criteria set out in the Convention have been met.[14] The Court can find that states have violated the Convention and, where it does, can award compensation to the victims and obliges the states in question to take certain measures of either an individual or general character.

The Convention enshrines essentially civil and political rights and freedoms. Since the adoption of the Convention, other rights have been added by means of different protocols (Nos. 1, 4, 6, 7, 12 and 13, ETS Nos. 9, 46, 114, 117, 177 and 187 respectively), but none contains an explicit right to the environment.

Nevertheless, the Court has emphasised that the effective enjoyment of the rights which are encompassed in the Convention depends notably on a sound, quiet and healthy environment conducive to well-being. The subject-matter of the cases examined by the Court shows that a range of environmental factors may have an impact on individual convention rights, such as noise levels from airports, industrial pollution, or town planning.

As environmental concerns have become more important nationally and internationally since 1950, the case-law of the Court has increasingly reflected the idea that human rights law and environmental law are mutually

---

13. Albania, Andorra, Armenia, Austria, Azerbaijan, Belgium, Bosnia and Herzegovina, Bulgaria, Croatia, Cyprus, Czech Republic, Denmark, Estonia, Finland, France, Georgia, Germany, Greece, Hungary, Iceland, Ireland, Italy, Latvia, Liechtenstein, Lithuania, Luxembourg, Malta, Moldova, Monaco, Montenegro, Netherlands, Norway, Poland, Portugal, Romania, Russian Federation, San Marino, Serbia, Slovakia, Slovenia, Spain, Sweden, Switzerland, "the former Yugoslav Republic of Macedonia", Turkey, Ukraine, United Kingdom.
14. Admissibility criteria are listed in Article 35 of the Convention.

reinforcing. Notably, the Court is not bound by its previous decisions, and in carrying out its task of interpreting the Convention, the Court adopts an evolutive approach. Therefore, the interpretation of the rights and freedoms is not fixed but can take account of the social context and changes in society.[15] As a consequence, even though no explicit right to a clean and quiet environment is included in the Convention or its protocols,[16] the case-law of the Court has shown a growing awareness of a link between the protection of the rights and freedoms of individuals and the environment. The Court has also made reference, in its case law, to other international environmental law standards and principles (see Appendix III).

However, it is not primarily upon the European Court of Human Rights to determine which measures are necessary to protect the environment, but upon national authorities. The Court has recognised that national authorities are best placed to make decisions on environmental issues, which often have difficult social and technical aspects. Therefore, in reaching its judgments, the Court affords the national authorities in principle a wide discretion – in the language of the Court a wide "margin of appreciation" – in their decision-making in this sphere. This is the practical implementation of the principle of subsidiarity, which has been stressed in the Interlaken Declaration of the High Level Conference on the Future of the European Court of Human Rights.[17] According to this principle, violations of the Convention should be prevented or remedied at the national level with the Court intervening only as a last resort. The principle is particularly important in the context of environmental matters due to their very nature.

The following section is solely dedicated to the Court's case-law.[18] It will describe the scope of environmental protection based on Articles 2, 6 (1), 8, 10, 13 and Article 1 of Protocol No. 1 of the Convention.[19] At first it will discuss which substantial rights based on the right to life (Chapter I), the right to respect for private and family life (Chapter II) and the right to protection

---

15. The Court often refers to the Convention as a "living instrument".
16. *Hatton and Others v. the United Kingdom* [GC], judgment of 8 July 2003, paragraph 96; *Dubetska and Others v. Ukraine*, judgment of 10 February 2011, also *Ioan Marchiş and Others v. Romania*, decision of 28 June 2011, paragraph 28.
17. Preamble part PP6 and paragraph 2 of the Interlaken Declaration of 19 February 2010, available at: www.eda.admin.ch/etc/medialib/downloads/edazen/topics/europa/euroc.Par.0133.File.tmp/final_en.pdf.
18. The section only considers case-law of the Court up to July 2011. However, Appendix II includes also more recent jurisprudence.
19. For reference to Article 3 ECHR see footnote 1.

of property (Chapter III). Thereafter, procedural rights relating to information and communication (Chapter IV), decision-making procedure (Chapter V) and the access to justice and other remedies (Chapter VI). Finally some general remarks on the territorial scope of the application of the Convention are made (Chapter VII).

More information regarding the Convention and the Court and notably the full text of the Convention as well as the practical conditions to lodge an application with the Court are to be found on the Court's website at: www.echr.coe.int/echr/. There is also a database (HUDOC) providing the full text of all the judgments of the Court and most of its decisions at: www.echr.coe.int/echr/en/hudoc.

Chapter I: Right to life and the environment

ARTICLE 2
RIGHT TO LIFE

1. Everyone's right to life shall be protected by law. No one shall be deprived of his life intentionally save in the execution of a sentence of a court following his conviction of a crime for which this penalty is provided by law.

2. Deprivation of life shall not be regarded as inflicted in contravention of this article when it results from the use of force which is no more than absolutely necessary:

   – in defence of any person from unlawful violence;
   – in order to effect a lawful arrest or to prevent the escape of a person lawfully detained;
   – in action lawfully taken for the purpose of quelling a riot or insurrection.

(a) The right to life is protected under Article 2 of the Convention. This Article does not solely concern deaths resulting directly from the actions of the agents of a State, but also lays down a positive obligation on States to take appropriate steps to safeguard the lives of those within their jurisdiction.[20] This means that public authorities have a duty to take steps to guarantee the rights of the Convention even when they are threatened by other (private) persons or activities that are not directly connected with the State.

1. The primary purpose of Article 2 is to prevent the State from deliberately taking life, except in the circumstances it sets out. This provision is negative in character, it aims to stop certain State actions. However, the Court has developed in its jurisprudence the "*doctrine of positive obligations*". This means that in some situations Article 2 may also impose on public authorities a duty to take steps to guarantee the right to life when it is threatened by persons or activities not directly connected with the State. For example, the police should prevent individuals about to carry out life-threatening acts against other individuals from doing so, and the legislature should make a criminal offence of any action of individuals deliberately leading to the loss of life. The Court's case-law has shown that this obligation is not limited to law enforcement agencies. Given the fundamental importance of the right to life and the fact that most infringements are irreversible, this positive obligation of protection can apply in situations where life is at risk. In the context of the environment, Article 2 has been applied where certain activities endangering the environment are so dangerous that they also endanger human life.

2. It is not possible to give an exhaustive list of examples of situations in which this obligation might arise. It must be stressed however that cases in which issues under Article 2 have arisen are exceptional. So far, the Court has considered environmental issues in four cases brought under Article 2, two of which relate to dangerous activities and two which relate to natural disasters. In theory, Article 2 can apply even though loss of life has not occurred, for example in situations where potentially lethal force is used inappropriately.[21]

---

20. *L.C.B. v. the United Kingdom*, judgment of 9 June 1998, paragraph 36; *Paul and Audrey Edwards v. the United Kingdom*, judgment of 14 March 2002, paragraph 54; *Öneryıldız v. Turkey* [GC], judgment of 30 November 2004, paragraph 71; *Budayeva and Others v. Russia*, paragraph 128.
21. E.g. *Makaratzis v. Greece* [GC], judgment of 20 December 2004, paragraph 49.

(b) The Court has found that the positive obligation on States may apply in the context of dangerous activities, such as nuclear tests, the operation of chemical factories with toxic emissions or waste-collection sites, whether carried out by public authorities themselves or by private companies.[22] In general, the extent of the obligations of public authorities depends on factors such as the harmfulness of the dangerous activities and the foreseeability of the risks to life.[23]

3. In *L.C.B. v. the United Kingdom*, the applicant's father had been exposed to radiation whilst serving in the army during nuclear tests in the 1950s. The applicant herself was born in 1966. She later contracted leukaemia and alleged that the United Kingdom's failure to warn and advise her parents of the dangers of the tests to any children they might have, as well as the State's failure to monitor her health, were violations of the United Kingdom's duties under Article 2. The Court considered that its task was to determine whether the State had done all that could be required of it to prevent the applicant's life from being avoidably put at risk.[24] It held that the United Kingdom would only have been required to act on its own motion to advise her parents and monitor her health if, on the basis of the information available to the State at the time in question, it had appeared likely that exposure of her father to radiation might have caused a real risk to her health. In the instant case, the Court considered that the applicant had not established a causal link between the exposure of her father to radiation and her own suffering from leukaemia. The Court therefore concluded that it was not reasonable to hold that, in the late 1960s, the United Kingdom authorities, on the basis of this unsubstantiated link, could or should have taken action in respect of the applicant. The Court thus found that there was no violation of Article 2.

4. On the other hand, the Court found a violation of Article 2 in the case of *Öneryıldız v. Turkey*. In this case, an explosion occurred on a municipal rubbish tip, killing thirty-nine people who had illegally built their dwellings around it. Nine members of the applicant's family died in the accident. Although an expert report had drawn the attention of the municipal authorities to the danger of a methane

---

22. *Öneryıldız v. Turkey* [GC], paragraph 71.
23. *Öneryıldız v. Turkey* [GC], paragraph 73; *L.C.B. v. the United Kingdom*, paragraphs 37-41.
24. *L.C.B. v. the United Kingdom*, paragraphs 36 and 38.

explosion at the tip two years before the accident, the authorities had taken no action. The Court found that since the authorities knew – or ought to have known – that there was a real and immediate risk to the lives of people living near the rubbish tip, they had an obligation under Article 2 to take preventive measures to protect those people. The Court also criticised the authorities for not informing those living next to the tip of the risks they were running by living there. The regulatory framework in place was also considered to be defective.

(c) In addition, the Court requires States to discharge their positive obligation to prevent the loss of life also in cases of natural disasters, even though they are as such, beyond human control, in contrast to the case of dangerous activities where States are required to hold ready appropriate warning and defence mechanisms.[25]

5. In *Budayeva and Others v. Russia*, the Court was asked to consider whether Russia had failed its positive obligation to warn the local population, to implement evacuation and emergency relief policies or, after the disaster, to carry out a judicial enquiry, despite the foreseeable threat to the lives of its inhabitants in this hazardous area. The application resulted from a severe mudslide after heavy rain falls, which had cost numerous lives. The Court also found that there had been a causal link between the serious administrative flaws in this case and the applicants' death.

6. The earlier case of *Murillo Saldias v. Spain*[26] also supports the existence of such positive obligation in the event of natural disasters. In this case the applicants complained that the State had failed to comply with its positive obligation to take necessary preventive measures to forestall the numerous deaths that occurred during a flooding of a campsite following strong rain. The Court did not explicitly affirm a positive obligation, however it found that the applications were inadmissible not because the article did not apply *ratione materiae* to natural disasters, but because one of the applicants had already obtained satisfaction at the national level and that the remaining applicants had failed to exhaust the available domestic remedies.

---

25. *Budazeva and Others v. Russia*, judgment of 22 March 2008, paragraph 135.
26. *Murillo Saldias v. Spain*, decision of 28 November 2006.

(d) In the first place, public authorities may be required to take measures to prevent infringements of the right to life as a result of dangerous activities or natural disasters. This entails, above all, the primary duty of a State to put in place a legislative and administrative framework which includes: [27]

- making regulations which take into account the special features of a situation or an activity and the level of potential risk to life. In the case of dangerous activities this entails regulations that govern the licensing, setting-up, operation, security and supervision of such activities;[28]

- placing particular emphasis on the public's right to information concerning such activities. In cases of natural disasters this includes the maintenance of an adequate defence and warning infrastructure;[29]

- providing for appropriate procedures for identifying shortcomings in the technical processes concerned and errors committed by those responsible.[30]

7. In the *Öneryıldız* and *Budayeva* judgments the Court stated that this is the primary duty flowing from the positive obligation in Article 2. The legislative and administrative framework should provide effective deterrence against threats to the right to life. Although this has previously been applied in the context of law enforcement, the significance is that in both these cases, the Court transposes this principle to environmental hazards. In *Öneryıldız* the Court applies it in the context of dangerous activities and in *Budayeva* the Court applies it to natural disasters. Moreover, in the case of dangerous activities the significance of the necessary legislative and administrative framework will usually require that the responsible public authorities make regulations concerning dangerous activities. In modern industrial societies there will always be activities which are inherently risky. The Court said that regulation of such activities should make it compulsory for all those concerned to take practical measures to protect people whose lives might be endangered by the inherent risks.

---

27. *Öneryıldız v. Turkey* [GC], paragraph 89; *Budayeva and Others v. Russia*, paragraph 129.
28. *Öneryıldız v. Turkey* [GC], paragraph 90; *Budayeva and Others v. Russia*, paragraphs 129 and 132.
29. *Öneryıldız v. Turkey* [GC], paragraph 90; *Budayeva and Others v. Russia*, paragraphs 129 and 132.
30. *Öneryıldız v. Turkey* [GC], paragraph 90; *Budayeva and Others v. Russia*, paragraphs 129 and 132.

8. The most significant difference between cases of natural disasters and dangerous activities is that the Court tends to provide States with a broader margin of appreciation for the former due to their unforeseeable nature, which is beyond human control.[31] Moreover, the Court stated that:

the scope of the positive obligations imputable to the State in the particular circumstances would depend on the origin of the threat and the extent to which one or the other risk is susceptible to mitigation.

Accordingly, it held:

In the sphere of emergency relief, where the State is directly involved in the protection of human lives through the mitigation of natural hazards, these considerations should apply in so far as the circumstances of a particular case point to the imminence of a natural hazard that had been clearly identifiable, and especially where it concerned a recurring calamity affecting a distinct area developed for human habitation or use.[32]

(e) Secondly, where loss of life may be the result of an infringement of the right to life, the relevant public authorities must provide an adequate response, judicial or otherwise. They must ensure that the legislative and administrative framework is properly implemented and that breaches of the right to life are repressed and punished as appropriate.[33]

(f) This response by the State includes the duty to promptly initiate an independent and impartial investigation. The investigation must be capable of ascertaining the circumstances in which the incident took place and identifying shortcomings in the operation of the regulatory system. It must also be capable of identifying the public officials or authorities involved in the chain of events in issue.[34]

---

31. *Budayeva and Others v. Russia*, paragraphs 134-135.
32. *Budayeva and Others v. Russia*, paragraph 137.
33. *Öneryıldız v. Turkey* [GC], paragraph 91; *Budayeva and Others v. Russia*, paragraph 138.
34. *Öneryıldız v. Turkey* [GC], paragraph 94; *Budayeva and Others v. Russia*, paragraph 142.

(g) If the infringement of the right to life is not intentional, civil, administrative or even disciplinary remedies may be a sufficient response.[35] However, the Court has found that, in particular in the case of dangerous activities, where the public authorities were fully aware of the likely consequences and disregarded the powers vested in them, hence failing to take measures that are necessary and sufficient to avert certain risks which might involve loss of life, Article 2 may require that those responsible for endangering life be charged with a criminal offence or prosecuted.[36]

9. The obligations which public authorities have in relation to the right to life are not just preventive; they do not just have the obligation to do their best to ensure that human life is protected. When life is lost, they are also required to find out why it was lost, who was responsible and what lessons can be learned. This is sometimes referred to as the "procedural aspect" of Article 2 because it imposes on States investigative obligations after the loss of life occurred. The aim of such obligation is to ensure that the legislative and administrative framework that is required to protect life does not exist on paper only. The Court also recognises that the victims' families have a right to know why their relatives have died and that society has an interest in punishing those responsible for the loss of human life.

10. The reason why public authorities are required to carry out an investigation is that they are usually the only bodies capable of identifying the causes of the incidents in question. The requirements that the investigation be prompt, independent and impartial seek to ensure its effectiveness. In *Öneryıldız v. Turkey*, where lives had been lost, the Court held that the authorities should of their own motion launch investigations into the accident which led to these deaths. It also found that in carrying out this investigation the competent authorities must first find out why the regulatory framework in place did not work, and secondly identify those officials or authorities involved in whatever capacity in the chain of events leading to the loss of life.

---

35. *Öneryıldız v. Turkey* [GC], paragraph 92; *Budayeva and Others v. Russia*, paragraph 139.
36. *Öneryıldız v. Turkey* [GC], paragraph 93; *Budayeva and Others v. Russia*, paragraph 140.

11. Furthermore, the Court emphasised in the Öneryıldız case that Article 2 does not automatically entail the right for an individual to have those responsible prosecuted or sentenced for a criminal offence. In cases where life has been lost, the need to deter future failure may in certain situations require criminal prosecution of those who are responsible in order to comply with Article 2, for instance where the taking of human life is intentional. However, in the specific field of environmental risks, loss of life is more likely to be unintentional. In such cases, States do not automatically have to prosecute those responsible. For example, where the loss of life was the result of human error or carelessness other less severe penalties may be imposed. However, in *Öneryıldız v. Turkey* the Court found that where the public authorities knew of certain risks, and knew that the consequences of not taking action to reduce those risks could lead to the loss of life, then the State may be under an obligation to prosecute those responsible for criminal offences. This may be the case even where there are other possibilities for taking action against those responsible (e.g. by initiating administrative or disciplinary proceedings).

12. The above principles developed with respect to dangerous activities have also been transposed by the Court in *Budayeva and Others v. Russia* and *Murillo Saldias and Others v. Spain* to situations of disaster relief.

Chapter II: Respect for private and family life as well as well as the home and the environment

ARTICLE 8
RIGHT TO RESPECT FOR PRIVATE AND FAMILY LIFE

1. Everyone has the right to respect for his private and family life, his home and his correspondence.

2. There shall be no interference by a public authority with the exercise of this right except such as is in accordance with the law and is necessary in a democratic society in the interests of national security, public safety or the economic well-being of the country, for the prevention of disorder or crime, for the protection of health or morals, or for the protection of the rights and freedoms of others.

(a) The right to respect for private and family life and the home are protected under Article 8 of the Convention. This right implies respect for the quality of private life as well as the enjoyment of the amenities of one's home ("living space").[37]

> 13. In a number of cases the Court has found that severe environmental pollution can affect people's well-being and prevent them from enjoying their homes to such an extent that their rights under Article 8 are violated. According to the Court the right to respect for the home does not only include the right to the actual physical area, but also to the quiet enjoyment of this area within reasonable limits. Therefore, breaches of this right are not necessarily confined to obvious interferences such as an unauthorised entry into a person's home, but may also result from intangible sources such as noise, emissions, smells or other similar forms of interference.[38] If such interferences prevent a person from enjoying the amenities of this home that person's right to respect for his home may be breached. In the context of cases raising issues linked to environmental degradation or nuisance the Court has tended to interpret the notions of private and family life and home as being closely interconnected, and, for example, in one case it referred to the notion of "private sphere"[39] or in another case "living space".[40] A "home", according to the Court's rather broad notion, is the place, i.e. physically defined area, where private and family life develops.

(b) Environmental degradation does not necessarily involve a violation of Article 8 as it does not include an express right to environmental protection or nature conservation.[41]

(c) For an issue to arise under Article 8, the environmental factors must directly and seriously affect private and family life or the home. Thus, there are two issues which the Court must consider – whether a causual link exists between the activity and the negative impact on the individual and whether the adverse have attained a certain threshold

---

37. *Powell & Rayner v. the United Kingdom*, judgment of 21 February 1990, paragraph 40.
38. *Moreno Gómez v. Spain*, judgment of 16 November 2004, paragraph 53; *Borysiewicz v. Poland*, judgment of 1 July 2008, paragraph 48; *Giacomelli v. Italy*, judgment of 2 November 2006, paragraph 76; *Hatton and Others v. the United Kingdom* [GC], judgment of 8 July 2003, paragraph 96; *Deés v. Hungary*, judgment of 9 November 2010, paragraph 21.
39. *Fadeyeva v. Russia*, judgment of 9 June 2005, paragraphs 70, 82 and 86.
40. *Brânduşe v. Romania,* paragraph 64 "l'espace de vie".
41. *Fadeyeva v. Russia*, paragraph 68; *Kyrtatos v. Greece*, judgment of 22 May 2003, paragraph 52; *Dubetska and Others v. Ukraine*, paragraph 105.

of harm. The assessment of that minimum threshold depends on all the circumstances of the case, such as the intensity and duration of the nuisance and its physical or mental effects, as well as on the general environmental context.[42]

14. It should first be recalled that environmental factors may raise an issue under Article 8 and trigger its applicability without the Court necessarily finding a violation of the Convention afterwards. Indeed, the Court starts its examination of a case by determining whether or not Article 8 is applicable to the circumstances of the case (i.e. whether or not the problem raised comes within the scope of Article 8), and only if it finds it to be applicable does it examine whether or not there has been a violation of this provision.

15. In the *Kyrtatos v. Greece*[43] case, the applicants brought a complaint under Article 8 alleging that urban development had led to the destruction of a swamp adjacent to their property, and that the area around their home had lost its scenic beauty. The Court emphasised that domestic legislation and certain other international instruments rather than the Convention are more appropriate to deal with the general protection of the environment. The purpose of the Convention is to protect individual human rights, such as the right to respect for the home, rather than the general aspirations or needs of the community taken as a whole. The Court highlighted in this case that

neither Article 8 nor any of the other articles of the Convention are specifically designed to provide general protection of the environment as such.[44]

In this case, the Court found no violation of Article 8.

16. On the other hand, the Court has found that "severe environmental pollution" such as excessive noise levels generated by an airport,[45] fumes, smells and contamination emanating from a waste treatment plant[46] and

---

42. *Fadeyeva v. Russia*, paragraph 69.
43. *Kyrtatos v. Greece*, judgment of 22 May 2003.
44. *Kyrtatos v. Greece*, paragraph 52.
45. *Hatton and Others v. the United Kingdom* [GC].
46. *López Ostra v. Spain*, judgment of 9 December 1994; *Giacomelli v. Italy.*

toxic emissions from a factory[47] can interfere with a person's peaceful enjoyment of his or her home in such a way as to raise an issue under Article 8, even when the pollution is not seriously health threatening.[48]

17. In *Leon and Agnieszka Kania v. Poland* [49] the Court had to consider whether the long proceedings to close a private company which emitted high levels of noise violated Article 8. The Court first reiterated that

there is no explicit right in the Convention to a clean and quiet environment, but that where an individual is directly and seriously affected by noise or other pollution, an issue may arise under Article 8.

Nevertheless, the Court concluded that it had not been established that the noise levels considered in the present case were so serious as to reach the high threshold established in cases dealing with environmental issues. Therefore, the Court held that Article 8 of the Convention had not been violated.

18. In contrast, in the *López Ostra v. Spain* case, the applicant complained that the fumes and noise from a waste treatment plant situated near her home made her family's living conditions unbearable. After having had to bear the nuisance caused by the plant for more than three years, the family moved elsewhere when it became clear that the nuisance could go on indefinitely and when her daughter's paediatrician recommended them to relocate. The national authorities, while recognising that the noise and smells had a negative effect on the applicant's quality of life, argued that they did not constitute a grave health risk and that they did not reach a level of severity breaching the applicant's fundamental rights. However, the Court found that severe environmental pollution may affect individuals' well-being and prevent them from enjoying their homes in such a way as to affect adversely their private and family life, even though it does not seriously endanger their health. In this case, the Court found a violation of Article 8.

19. Likewise, in *Brânduşe v. Romania* the Court did not require an actual impact on the health of the applicant to find Article 8 applicable.[50] In the case the Court was required to determine firstly whether Article 8 of the Convention applied in the case of an applicant who considered the cell in which he was serving a prison sentence to be his "living space", and

---

47. *Guerra and Others v. Italy* [GC], judgment of 19 February 1998; *Tătar v. Romania*, judgment of 27 January 2009 (in French only); *Ledyayeva and Others v. Russia*, judgment of 26 October 2006; *Fadeyeva v. Russia*.
48. *Taşkın and Others v. Turkey*, judgment of 10 November 2004, paragraph 113; *Ioan Marchiş and Others v. Romania*, paragraph 28.
49. *Leon and Agnieszka Kania v. Poland,* judgment of 21 July 2009, paragraphs 98-104.
50. *Brânduşe v. Romania*, paragraph 67.

secondly whether the bad odours from a nearby rubbish tip breached the gravity threshold to fall within the scope of Article 8. The Court agreed with the applicant that Article 8 applied to his cell as the cell represented the only "living space" available to the prisoner for several years. Moreover, the Court clearly held that the quality of life and well-being of the applicant had been affected in a manner that had impaired his private life and was not just the consequence of the deprivation of his liberty. Thereby it found that the pure absence of any health impact is not sufficient alone to dismiss the applicability of Article 8. In the end the Court found a violation of this article.

20. Another example is the *Fadeyeva v. Russia* case. In this case the applicant lived in the vicinity of a steel plant. The Court observed that in order to fall under Article 8, complaints relating to environmental nuisances have to show, firstly, that there has been an actual interference with the individual's "private sphere", and, secondly, that these nuisances have reached a certain level of severity. In the case in question, the Court found that over a significant period of time the concentration of various toxic elements in the air near the applicant's house seriously exceeded safe levels and that the applicant's health had deteriorated as a result of the prolonged exposure to the industrial emissions from the steel plant. Therefore, the Court accepted that the actual detriment to the applicant's health and well-being reached a level sufficient to bring it within the scope of Article 8 of the Convention. Here the Court concluded that there had been a violation of Article 8.

21. In *Dubetska and Others v. Ukraine*, like in *Fadeyeva v. Russia,* the Court stressed with regard to the minimum threshold necessary to invoke Article 8 that no issue will arise if the detriment complained of is negligible in comparison to the environmal hazards inherent in life in every modern city.[51] In *Dubetska and Others v. Ukraine* the applicants living in a rural area complained that they suffered chronic health problems and damage to their homes and the living environment as a result of a coal mine and a factory which were operated nearby. The Court recognised that while there is no doubt that industrial pollution may negatively affect public health in general and worsen the quality of an individual's life, it is often impossible to quantify its effect in each individual case. It is often hard to distinguish the effect of environmental hazards from the influence of other relevant factors. The Court further held that living in an area marked by pollution in clear excess of applicable safety standards exposed the applicants to an elevated risk to health. In the present case, the Court found that the specific area in which

---

51. *Dubetska and Others v. Ukraine*, paragraph 105; also *Ioan Marchiş and Others v. Romania*, paragraph 33.

the applicant lived was both according to the legislative framework (provision of minimum distances from industrial plants) and empirically unsafe for residual use. Consequently, the Court found a violation of Article 8 as the authorities had not found an effective solution to the applicants situation for 12 years either by curbing the pollution or resettling them as envisaged by national court judgments.[52]

22. In *Grimkovskaya v. Ukraine*, the Court reaffirmed that the hazard at issue necessary to raise a claim under Article 8 must attain a level of severity resulting in a "significant impartment if the applicant's ability to enjoy her home, private or family life" and that the assessment of all circumstances of the case is needed to decide on the threat level.[53] In this case, the Ukrainian authorities routed in 1998 a motorway through a street which had been constructed as a residential street. It had no drainage system, pavement or proper surfacing able to withstand high volumes of heavy goods traffic. In addition, potholes which appeared were occasionally filled up by the road authorities with cheap materials including waste from coal-mines which were high in heavy metal content. The applicant claimed that her house had become unusable and the people living in it suffered from constant vibrations provoked by the traffic and from noise and pollution. While the Court found that there was insufficient evidence to prove all the applicant's allegations (e.g. the detailed impact on the health of the inhabitants), it relied on evidence showing that in general the level of emissions was above the statutory limits and that some of the applicant's son's health issues could not be plausibly explained (e.g. lead and copper salts poisoning) to conclude that the

cumulative effect of noise, vibrations and air and soil pollution generated by the [...] motorway significantly deterred the applicant from enjoying her rights guaranteed by Article 8.[54]

However, the Court found a violation only with regard to procedural aspects of the decision-making and complaints procedure.

23. Yet, the case of *Tătar v. Romania* is also remarkable. In this case the applicants, who lived near a gold ore extraction plant, had lodged several complaints with the authorities about the risks to which they were being exposed because of the use by the company of a technical procedure involving sodium cyanide. In 2000, despite the fact that the authorities had reassured the applicant that sufficient safety mechanisms existed, a large quantity of polluted water spilled into various rivers, crossing

---

52. *Dubetska and Others v. Ukraine*, paragraphs 105-106, 111, 118.
53. *Grimkovskaya v. Ukraine*, paragraph 58.
54. *Grimkovskaya v. Ukraine*, paragraph 62.

several borders and affecting the environment of several countries. In this particular case the Court was confronted with the problem that there was no internal decision or other official document stating explicitly how much of a threat the company's activities posed to human health and the environment.[55] The Court noticed that the applicant failed to obtain any official document from the authorities confirming that the company's activities were dangerous. Moreover, the Court found that the applicants had failed to prove that there was a sufficient causal link between the pollution caused and the worsening of their symptoms. Nevertheless, on the basis of environmental impact studies of the spilling submitted by the respondent State, the Court concluded that a serious and substantial threat to the applicants' well-being existed. Consequently, the State was under a positive obligation to adopt reasonable and sufficient measures to protect the rights of the interested parties to respect for their private lives and their home and, more generally, a healthy, protected environment.[56] This applied to the authorities just as much before the plant had begun operating as after the accident.

24. In this respect it is notable that the Court emphasised the importance of the precautionary principle (which had been established for the first time by the Rio Declaration), whose purpose was to secure a high level of protection for the health and safety of consumers and the environment in all the activities of the Community.[57] It held that the national authorities' positive obligations to ensure respect for private and family life applied with even more force to the period after the accident of 2000.[58] The applicants must have lived in a state of anxiety and uncertainty, accentuated by the passive approach of the national authorities and compounded by the fear stemming from the continuation of the activity and the possibility that the accident might occur again. Consequently, the Court found that there had been a violation of Article 8 of the Convention.

25. However, the precautionary principle does not protect against every potential harm that is conceivable. In the case of *Luginbühl v. Switzerland*,[59] the applicant claimed that emissions caused by a mobile phone antenna could impact her health and so lead to a violation of Article 8 of the Convention. The Court noted that the Swiss authorities had published a scientific study on the effects of mobile phones on the environment and the health of individuals, and that the issue of the

---

55. *Tătar v. Romania*, paragraph 93.
56. *Tătar v. Romania*, paragraph 107.
57. *Tătar v. Romania*, paragraph 120.
58. *Tătar v. Romania*, paragraph 121.
59. *Luginbühl v. Switzerland*, decision of 17 January 2006.

noxiousness had not been proven scientifically for the time being. The Court concluded that the complaint under Article 8 should be rejected, as well as the complaint under Article 2 of the Convention. Hence, the Court requires at least some scientific validity of the claim that a certain activity is dangerous to the environment and/or health.

26. In addition, considering the *Taşkın and Others v. Turkey*[60] case, it appears that the Court has a two track approach to Article 8. In this case the Court was called upon whether national authorities had incorrectly prolonged the operation permit of a gold mine which was employing a particular technique that could have a negative impact on the environment and the applicant's health. On the one hand, if the possible environmental damage is severe enough that it seems likely that individuals' well-beings and the enjoyment of their homes are adversely affected, the Court refrains from a more in-depth analysis of the link between the pollution and the negative impact and the gravity of the impact on the individual. However, in case of "dangerous activities" the Court requires a "sufficiently close link" to be established with the private and family life of an applicant to accept the invocation of Article 8.

(d) While the objective of Article 8 is essentially that of protecting the individual against arbitrary interference by public authorities, it may also imply in some cases an obligation on public authorities to adopt positive measures designed to secure the rights enshrined in this article.[61] This obligation does not only apply in cases where environmental harm is directly caused by State activities but also when it results from private sector activities.[62] Public authorities must make sure that such measures are implemented so as to guarantee rights protected under Article 8.[63] The Court has furthermore explicitly recognised that public authorities may have a duty to inform the public about environmental risks.[64] Moreover, the Court has stated with regard to the scope of the positive obligation that it is generally irrelevant of whether a situation is assessed from the perspective of paragraph 1 of Article 8 which, *inter alia,* relates to the positive

---

60. *Taşkın and Others v. Turkey,* paragraph 113.
61. *Guerra and Others v. Italy* [GC], paragraph 58.
62. *Hatton and Others v. the United Kingdom* [GC], paragraph 98; *Tătar v. Romania,* paragraph 87; *Deés v. Hungary,* paragraph 21.
63. *Moreno Gómez v. Spain,* paragraph 61.
64. *Guerra and Others v. Italy* [GC], paragraph 60; *Tătar v. Romania,* paragraph 88; *Lemke v. Turkey,* judgment of 5 June 2007 (in French only), paragraph 41.

obligations of State authorities, or paragraph 2 asking whether a State interference was justified, as the principles applied are almost identical.[65]

27. According to the Court's case-law,[66] not only should public authorities refrain from interfering arbitrarily with individuals' rights, but they should also take active steps to safeguard these rights.[67] Such duties may arise also with regard to the relations between private parties.

28. In *Hatton and Others v. the United Kingdom*, which concerned aircraft noise generated by an international airport, the Court considered that whilst the activity was carried out by private parties Article 8 nonetheless applied because the State was responsible for properly regulating private industry in order to avoid or reduce noise pollution. In this case, the Court therefore concluded that the State had a responsibility to control air traffic and thus aircraft noise. However, the Court did not find a violation since, overall, the State could not be said to have failed to strike a fair balance between the interests of the complainants and the interests of others and of the community as a whole in the regulatory scheme it had put in place (see (e) below).

29. The *Moreno Gómez v. Spain* case concerned noise disturbance caused by discotheques and bars. The Spanish authorities were expected to take measures to keep noise disturbance at reasonable levels. Whilst they had made bylaws to set maximum noise levels and provided for the imposition of penalties and other measures on those who did not respect these levels, they failed to ensure that these measures were properly implemented. In this context, the Court stressed that the authorities should not only take measures aimed at preventing environmental disturbance, such as noise in the case at issue, but should also secure that these preventive measures are implemented in practice – thus ensuring their effectiveness in protecting the rights of individuals under Article 8. In this case the Court found a violation of Article 8.

30. Similarly, public authorities are expected to control emissions from industrial activities so that local residents do not suffer smells, noise or fumes emanating from nearby factories. An example illustrating this is the case of *Guerra and Others v. Italy*. In this case a chemical factory situated not far from where the applicants lived, was classified as high-risk. In the past, several accidents had occurred resulting in the hospitalisation of many people living nearby. The applicants did not complain of the action

---

65. *Guerra and Others v. Italy*, paragraph 60.
66. E.g. *Guerra and Others v. Italy* [GC].
67. The so-called "doctrine of positive obligations". *Hatton and Others v. the United Kingdom* [GC], paragraphs 100, 119, 123; *Dubetska and Others v. Ukraine*, paragraph 143.

of the public authorities, but, on the contrary, of their failure to act. The Court concluded that the public authorities had not fulfilled their obligation to secure the applicants' right to respect for their private and family life, on the ground that the applicants had not received essential information from the public authorities that would have enabled them to assess the risks which they and their families might run if they continued to live in the area. Here the Court ruled that there had been a violation of Article 8.

31. The case of *Ledyayeva and Others v. Russia*,[68] dealt with situation similar to the case of *Fadeyeva v. Russia*, in which the Court had found that the operation of a polluting steel plant in the middle of a densely populated town placed the State under an obligation to offer the applicant an effective solution to help her move away from the dangerous area or to reduce the toxic emissions. In the more recent Ledyayeva case the Court noted that the government had not put forward any new fact or argument that would persuade it to reach a conclusion different from that of the Fadeyeva case. Accordingly, the Court found that the Russian authorities had failed to take appropriate measures to protect the applicants' right to respect for their homes and their private lives against severe environmental nuisances. In particular, the authorities had not resettled the applicants outside the dangerous area or provided compensation for people seeking new accommodation. Nor had they devised and implemented an efficient policy to induce the owners of the steel plant to reduce its emissions to safe levels within a reasonable time. The Court found that there had been a violation of Article 8 of the Convention. With this judgment the Court underlined again its position from *Fadeyeva v. Russia* that a State's responsibility in cases relating to the environment "may arise from a failure to regulate [the] private industry."[69]

32. Moreover, in *Dubetska and Others v. Ukraine*[70] the Court applied the same principles regardless of the fact that the polluting state-owned factory was privatised in 2007. To determine whether or not the State could be held responsible under Article 8 of the Convention, the Court examined whether the situation was a result of a sudden and unexpected turn of events or, on the contrary, was long-standing and well known to the State authorities; whether the State was or should have been aware that the hazard or the nuisance was affecting the applicant's private life and to what extent the applicant contributed to creating this situation for himself and was in a position to remedy it without a prohibitive outlay.[71]

---

68. *Ledyayeva and Others v. Russia*, judgment of 26 October 2006.
69. *Fadeyeva v. Russia*, paragraph 89.
70. For a short description of this case, see paragraph 21 of the manual.
71. *Dubetska and Others v. Ukraine*, paragraph 108.

33. The case of *Deés v. Hungary* underlines the extent of the obligation to remedy violation resulting from a private third party. In this case, the volume of traffic routed through the applicant's town increased substantially in 1997 because of the attempt of many trucks to avoid rather high toll charges which had recently been introduced on a neighbouring, privately owned motorway. The government was aware of the increased burden on the citizens and tried to remedy it as early as 1998 through several measures including the construction of three bypass roads, a 40 km/h speed limit at night, the erection of several traffic lights and, in 2001, a ban of vehicles of over 6 tons on the town's road. Those measures were enforced through the increased presence of the police. Nevertheless, the Court found that the authorities failed in their duty to stop the third-party breaches of the right relied on by the applicant, since the measures taken consistently proved to be insufficient and, consequently, the applicant was consistently exposed to excessive noise disturbance over a substantial period of time. The Court held that this created a disproportionate individual burden for the applicant. Hence, it found a breach of Article 8.

34. However, in *Grimkovskaya v. Ukraine* the Court did not find a violation of Article 8 because the nuisances caused by the noise and pollution emitted from a nearby motorway were not effectively remedied by the authorities. It recognised the complexity of States' task in handling infrastructural issues holding that Article 8 cannot be constructed as requiring States to ensure that every individual enjoys housing that meets particular environmental standards. Consequently, it would be going too far to render the government responsible for the very fact of allowing cross-town traffic to pass through a populated street or establish the applicants right to free, new housing at the State's expense, especially since the applicant had not proven that she could not relocate without the State's help. Nevertheless, the Court found a violation of the procedural obligations of Article 8 because minimal safeguards had not been respected by the authorities. The Court considered that, *inter alia*, the efficient and meaningful management of the street through a reasonable policy aimed at mitigating the motorway's harmful effects on the Article 8 right of the street's residents belonged to those minimal safeguards (see also chapter V).[72]

35. With regard to the authorities' obligation to inform the public on environmental matters, see chapter IV.

---

72. *Grimkovskaya v. Ukraine*, paragraphs 65-66, 68, 73.

(e) Where decisions of public authorities affect the environment to the extent that there is an interference with the right to respect for private or family life or the home, they must accord with the conditions set out in Article 8 paragraph 2.[73] Such decisions must thus be provided for by law and follow a legitimate aim, such as the economic well-being of the country or the protection of the rights and freedoms of others. In addition, they must be proportionate to the legitimate aim pursued: for this purpose, a fair balance must be struck between the interest of the individual and the interest of the community as a whole.[74] Since the social and technical aspects of environmental issues are often difficult to assess, the relevant public authorities are best placed to determine what might be the best policy.[75] Therefore they enjoy in principle a wide margin of appreciation in determining how the balance should be struck.[76] The Court may nevertheless assess whether the public authorities have approached the problem with due diligence and have taken all the competing interests into consideration.[77]

36. The Convention recognises that the obligation of the State not to take measures which interfere with private and family life or the home is not absolute. Therefore, in certain situations, interference by public authorities may be acceptable under the Convention. However, it has to be justified.

37. First, the interference must be in accordance with the law and the relevant law must be accessible and its effects foreseeable. In most of the relevant cases pertaining to the environment in which the Court has found a violation of Article 8, the breach did not result from the absence of legislation protecting the environment, but rather the failure of the authorities to respect such legislation. For instance, in *López Ostra v. Spain*[78] the operation of the waste-treatment plant was illegal because it was run without the necessary licence. In *Guerra and Others v. Italy* [79] the

---

73. *Hatton and Others v. the United Kingdom* [GC], paragraph 98.
74. *López Ostra v. Spain*, paragraph 51; *Öckan and Others v. Turkey*, paragraph 43.
75. *Powell and Rayner v. the United Kingdom*, paragraph 44; *Giacomelli v. Italy*, paragraph 80.
76. *Hatton and Others v. the United Kingdom* [GC], paragraphs 97, 98 and 100.
77. *Fadeyeva v. Russia*, paragraph 128.
78. For a short description of this case, see paragraph 18 of the manual.
79. For a short description of this case, see paragraph 30 of the manual.

applicants were unable to obtain information from the public authorities despite the existence of a national statutory obligation. Likewise, in *Taşkın and Others v. Turkey*[80] and *Fadeyeva and Others v. Russia*[81] the Court found violations because industrial activities were conducted illegally or in violation of existing national environmental standards. In *Fadeyeva v. Russia* the Court explicitly expounded that "in accordance with the law" means that "[a] breach of domestic law [...] would necessarily lead to a finding of a violation of the Convention."[82] In contrast, in *Hatton and Others v. the United Kingdom*[83] there was no such element of irregularity under United Kingdom law and the applicants did not contest that the interference with their right accorded with relevant national law. In any event the Court has tended to look at the question of the lawfulness of the actions of public authorities as a factor to be weighed among others in assessing whether a fair balance has been struck in accordance with Article 8 paragraph 2 and not as a separate and conclusive test.[84]

38. The interference must also follow a legitimate aim serving the interests of the community such as the economic well-being of the country.[85] Even then, there is an additional requirement that the measures taken by the authorities be proportionate to the aim pursued. In order to assess the proportionality of the measures taken, the Court will assess whether a fair balance has been struck between the competing interests of the community and the individuals concerned. In this context, the public authorities enjoy a certain flexibility – in the words of the Court, a "margin of appreciation"– in determining the steps to be taken to ensure compliance with the Convention. Since many aspects of the environment belong to a social and technical sphere that is difficult to assess, the Court acknowledges that national authorities are better placed than the Court itself to decide on the best policy to adopt in given circumstances. On the basis of this assumption, States therefore enjoy a certain leeway ("margin of appreciation") as to the measures which they may adopt to tackle detrimental environmental factors. The Court will take account of this margin of appreciation when it reviews whether a fair balance has been struck between the competing interests. These principles are applicable in a similar way in cases where the question

---

80. For a short description of this case, see paragraph 26 of the manual.
81. For a short description of this case, see paragraph 20 of the manual.
82. *Fadeyeva v. Russia*, paragraph 95. Moreover, in *López Ostra v. Spain* and *Taşkın and Others v. Turkey* national courts had already ordered the facilities to be closed, which was not implemented.
83. For a short description of this case, see paragraph 28 of the manual.
84. *Fadeyeva v. Russia*, paragraph 98.
85. E.g. the running of an international airport: *Powell and Rayner v. the United Kingdom* and *Hatton and Others v. the United Kingdom* [GC].

arises of whether the State has a positive obligation to take measures to secure the individual's right under paragraph 1 of Article 8.[86] In such instances, the measures taken by the authorities must also be in accordance with the law, proportionate and reasonable.

39. For example, in *López Ostra v. Spain* concerning the operation of a waste-treatment plant and its impact on the nearby inhabitants, the Court concluded that the State had not struck a fair balance between the interest of the town's economic well-being in having a waste-treatment plant and that of the applicant and her family's living conditions and health, i.e. the effective enjoyment of her right to respect for her home and her private and family life, which were drastically affected by the waste treatment plant's operation. In the case of *Fadeyeva v. Russia*,[87] the Court also concluded that despite the wide margin of appreciation left to the State, the Russian authorities had failed to strike a fair balance between the interests of the community and the applicant's effective enjoyment of her rights under Article 8, leading to a violation of this provision. In this respect the Court noted that the public authorities had not offered the applicant any effective solution to help her move away from the dangerous area and there was no information that the public authorities had designed or applied effective measures to stop the polluting steel plant from operating in breach of domestic environmental standards.[88]

40. In contrast, the wide margin of appreciation allowed the United Kingdom to sufficiently balance the environmental impact of the extension of Heathrow Airport against its economic gains. The Court found in *Hatton and Others v. the United Kingdom* that the additional night flight would not violate Article 8 because their frequency had been regulated, the environmental impact had been assessed in advance and measures such as sound-proofing houses had been taken.

41. In *Giacomelli v. Italy* the Court clearly set out in which respect it assesses whether States have acted within their margin of appreciation.[89] In the case the applicant complained of the noise and harmful emissions from a waste storage and treatment plant. The Court considered, recalling the cases of *Hatton and Others v. the United Kingdom* and *Taskin and Others v. Turkey*[90] that there were two aspects to the examination which it could carry out. Firstly, it could assess the substantive merits of the government's decision to authorise the plant to operate to ensure that it was compatible with Article 8. Secondly, it could

---

86. *López Ostra v. Spain*, paragraph 51; *Borysiewicz v. Poland*, judgment of 1 July 2008, paragraph 50.
87. For a short description of this case, see paragraph 20 of the manual.
88. *Fadeyeva v. Russia*, paragraphs 133 and 134.
89. *Giacomelli v. Italy*, paragraph 79.
90. *Taşkın and Others v. Turkey,* paragraph 15.

assess the decision-making process to check that due regard had been given to the individual's interests. With regard to the substantive aspect, the Court stressed that the State had to be granted a wide margin of appreciation and that it was primarily for the national authorities to assess the necessity of interference, although the decision-making process leading to the interference had to be fair and show due regard for the interests of the individual protected by Article 8.[91] Consequently, the Court considered the type of policy or decision involved, the extent to which the views of individuals were taken into account throughout the decision-making process, and the procedural safeguards available.[92] Nevertheless, the Court further stated that this does not prevent authorities from making decisions, e.g. providing operating licences, if they do not possess measureable data for each and every aspect of a project.[93]

42. Accordingly, in *Giacomelli v. Italy* the Court criticised the whole decision-making process whereby the waste treatment plant had been set up and operated. It noted that it had been impossible for citizens concerned to take part in the licensing procedure and make their own submissions to the judicial authorities and, where appropriate, obtain an order for the suspension of the dangerous activity. Even supposing that, much later, the measures required to protect the applicant's rights had been taken, the fact remained that for several years her right to respect for her home had been seriously impaired by the dangerous activities of the plant built thirty metres from her house.[94]

43. The Court's position on States' margin of appreciation has been reaffirmed also in the cases of *Öckan and Others v. Turkey*[95] and *Lemke v. Turkey*[96] in which the Court found that there had been a violation of Article 8 because of the threat posed to the applicants' health by the operations of a gold mine using cyanidation.[97] Here again the Court emphasised the importance of proper decision-making processes, including appropriate surveys and studies, which had to be accessible to the public (on this point, see chapters IV and V below).

---

91. See, *mutatis mutandis, McMichael v. the United Kingdom*, judgment of 24 February 1995, paragraph 87.
92. See also *Hatton and Others v. the United Kingdom* [GC], paragraph 104.
93. *Giacomelli v. Italy*, paragraph 82.
94. *Giacomelli v. Italy*, paragraph 96.
95. *Öckan and Others v. Turkey*, judgment of 28 March 2006.
96. *Lemke v. Turkey*, judgment of 5 June 2007 (in French only).
97. Identical circumstances to those of the case *Taşkın and Others v. Turkey*, judgment of 10 November 2004, already mentioned in the manual.

44. Likewise, did the Court find a violation of Article 8 in *Băcilă v. Romania*? In this case an applicant complained about the emissions of a lead and zinc plant in the town of Copşa Mică. Analyses carried out by public and private bodies established that heavy metals could be found in the town's waterways, in the air, in the soil and in vegetation, at levels of up to twenty times the maximum permitted. The rate of illness, particularly respiratory conditions, was seven times higher in Copşa Mică than in the rest of the country. The Court found that the authorities had failed to strike a fair balance between the public interest in maintaining the economic activity of the biggest employer in a town (the lead and zinc plant) and the applicant's effective enjoyment of the right to respect for her home and for her private and family life.[98]

45. The *Dubetska and Others v. Ukraine* case highlights the relationship between the margin of appreciation awarded to States and the requirement to strike a fair balance when weighing different interests. On the one hand the Court reaffirmed the State's margin of appreciation. For instance, the Court stated that it would be going too far to establish an applicant's general right to free new housing at the State's expense as the complaint under Article 8 could also be remedied by duly addressing the environmental hazards. On the other hand, it reiterated that the Convention is thought to protect effective rights and not illusory ones; therefore, the striking of a fair balance between the various interests at stake may be upset, not only where the regulations to protect guaranteed rights are lacking, but also where they are not duly complied with.

46. In the present case the Court found a violation of Article 8 because the government's approach to tackling pollution has been marked by numerous delays and inconsistent enforcement as well as the fact that the applicants were not resettled despite being only a few in number. In summary, the Court did not require a specific state action, but it required that the measures taken were effective in ceasing an interference in an individuals rights.[99]

47. Another interesting statement in the present case, alike to *Fadeyeva v. Russia,* relates to the burden of proof of the State when justifying an interference with an individual's right for the benefit of the general public. The Court held that "the onus is on the State to justify, using detailed and rigorous data, a situation in which certain individuals bear a heavy burden on behalf of the rest of the community."[100]

---

98. *Băcilă v. Romania*, judgment of 30 March 2010.
99. *Dubetska and Others. v. Ukraine*, paragraphs 143-145, 150-152, 155.
100. *Dubetska and Others. v. Ukraine*, paragraphs 145; *Fadeyeva and Others v. Russia*, paragraph 128.

(f) In addition, the Court has recognised the preservation of the environment, in particular in the framework of planning policies, as a legitimate aim justifying certain restrictions by public authorities on a person's right to respect for private and family life and the home.[101]

48. As explained earlier, the Convention provides protection when the right to respect for private and family life and for the home are breached as a result of environmental degradation. However, in some cases the protection of the environment can also be a legitimate aim allowing the authorities to restrict this right. In *Chapman v. the United Kingdom* the authorities refused to allow the applicant, a gypsy, to remain in a caravan on land which she owned on the ground that this plot was situated in an area which, according to the planning policies in force, was to be preserved and where, for this purpose, dwellings were prohibited. The Court found that, whilst the authorities' refusal interfered with the applicant's right to respect for private and family life and home (notably because of her lifestyle as a gypsy), it nevertheless pursued the legitimate aim of protecting the rights of others through preservation of the environment, and was proportionate to that aim. The Court thus concluded that Article 8 of the Convention had not been violated.

49. Notwithstanding the fact that they pursue the legitimate aim of preserving the environment, any restrictions by the authorities should meet the same requirements as with other legitimate aims (see paragraphs 36 to 38).[102]

---

101. *Chapman v. the United Kingdom* [GC], judgment of 18 January 2001, paragraph 82.

102. *Chapman v. the United Kingdom* [GC], paragraphs 90-91.

Chapter III: Protection of property and the environment

ARTICLE 1 OF PROTOCOL NO. 1
PROTECTION OF PROPERTY

Every natural or legal person is entitled to the peaceful enjoyment of his possessions. No one shall be deprived of his possessions except in the public interest and subject to the conditions provided for by law and by the general principles of international law.

The preceding provisions shall not, however, in any way impair the right of a State to enforce such laws as it deems necessary to control the use of property in accordance with the general interest or to secure the payment of taxes or other contributions or penalties.

(a) Under Article 1 of Protocol No. 1 to the Convention, individuals are entitled to the peaceful enjoyment of their possessions, including protection from unlawful deprivation of property. This provision does not, in principle, guarantee the right to continue to enjoy those possessions in a pleasant environment.[103] Article 1 of Protocol No. 1 also recognises that public authorities are entitled to control the use of property in accordance with the general interest.[104] In this context the Court has found that the environment is an increasingly important consideration.

50. The concept of "possessions" referred to in the Protocol has an autonomous meaning which is not limited to the ownership of physical goods and is independent from the formal classification in domestic law: certain other rights and interests constituting assets can also be regarded as "property rights", and thus as "possessions" for the purpose of this Convention. It always needs to be examined whether the circumstances of the case, considered as a whole, confer on the applicant a title to a substantive interest protected by Article 1 of Protocol No. 1.[105] The concept is not limited to existing possessions

---

103. *Taşkın and Others v. Turkey,* decision of 29 January 2004, "law" part (available in French only).
104. *Fredin v. Sweden,* judgment of 18 February 1991, paragraph 41.
105. *Iatridis v. Greece* [GC], judgment of 25 March 1999, paragraph 54; *Öneryıldız v. Turkey* [GC], judgment of 30 November 2004, paragraph 124; *Hamer v. Belgium,* paragraph 75; *Depalle v. France* [GC] , paragraph 62; *Brosset-Triboulet and Others v. France* [GC], paragraph 65.

but may also cover assets, including claims, in respect of which the applicant can argue that he or she has at least a reasonable and legitimate expectation of obtaining effective enjoyment of a property right.[106] A legitimate expectation of being able to continue having peaceful enjoyment of a property right of a possession must have a "sufficient basis in national law".[107]

51. Article 1 of Protocol No. 1 guarantees the right to the peaceful enjoyment of one's possessions. This right, however, is not absolute and certain restrictions are permissible. In certain circumstances, public authorities may order deprivation of property. However, any deprivation of one's property must be justified as being based on law and carried out in the public interest and a fair balance must be struck between the individual's interest and the public interest.[108] In assessing whether a fair balance has been struck, the payment of compensation to the individual concerned is of relevance. In other cases, public authorities may also impose restrictions on the right to the peaceful enjoyment of one's possessions which amount to a control of their use, provided that such control is lawful, in accordance with the public interest and proportionate.

52. The Court has found that the above-mentioned general features of Article 1 of Protocol No. 1 apply in cases raising environmental issues based on the premise that the protection of one's possession needs to be "practical and effective". However, the Court has held that Article 1 of Protocol No. 1 docs not necessarily secure a right to continue to enjoy one's property in a pleasant environment. On the other hand, it has also noted that certain activities which could affect the environment adversely could seriously reduce the value of a property to the extent of even making it impossible to sell it, thus amounting to a partial expropriation, or limiting its use creating a situation of *de facto* expropriation. Therefore the Court attempts to look behind the appearance and investigate the realities of the situation in question.[109]

---

106. *Hamer v. Belgium*, paragraph 75; *Depalle v. France* [GC], paragraph 63; *Brosset-Triboulet and Others v. France* [GC], paragraph 66.

107. *Kopecký v. Slovakia*, judgment of 28 September 2004, paragraph 52; *Brosset-Triboulet and Others v. France*, paragraphs 66, Cf. Concurring Opinion of Judge Casadevall, paragraph 3; *Depalle v. France* [GC], paragraph 63.

108. *Brosset-Triboulet and Others v. France* [GC], paragraph 80.

109. *Taşkın and Others v. Turkey*, decision of 29 January 2004, "law" part (available in French only).

(b) The general interest in the protection of the environment can justify certain restrictions by public authorities on the individual right to the peaceful enjoyment of one's possessions.[110] Such restrictions should be lawful and proportionate to the legitimate aim pursued. Public authorities enjoy a wide margin of appreciation in deciding with regard both to the choice of the means of enforcement and to the ascertaining whether the consequences of enforcement are justified in the general interest.[111] However, the measures taken by public authorities must be proportionate and strike a fair balance between the interests involved,[112] and here environmental preservation plays an increasingly important role.

53. Any restrictions by the public authorities on an individual's right to the peaceful enjoyment of his or her possessions must be in the general interest, i.e. in pursuit of a legitimate aim, which can be the protection of the environment. The Court has decided accordingly, for instance, with regard to the protection of the countryside, forests and the coastal areas. Measures taken in pursuit of such a legitimate aim must be in accordance with the law and the relevant law must be accessible and its effects foreseeable. Furthermore, the measures taken must be proportionate to the aim pursued, i.e. a fair balance must be struck between the individual and the general interests at stake. In assessing the fairness of this balance the Court recognises that the relevant national authorities are in a better position than the Court to judge how to weigh the various interests at stake. The Court therefore grants the State a "margin of appreciation", i.e. it will not seek to disturb the decision of the national authorities, unless the interference with the individual's rights is disproportionate. Additionally, the Court reiterated that regional planning and environmental conservation policies, where the community's general interest is pre-eminent, confer on the State a margin of appreciation that is greater than when exclusively civil rights are at stake.[113]

---

110. *Pine Valley Developments Ltd and Others v. Ireland*, judgment of 29 November 1991, paragraph 57.
111. *Fredin v. Sweden*, paragraph 51; *Z.A.N.T.E. – Marathonisi A.E. v. Greece*, judgment of 6 December 2007 (in French only) paragraph 50; *Brosset-Triboulet and Others v. France* [GC], paragraphs 81 and 86; *Depalle v. France* [GC], paragraph 83.
112. *Chapman v. the United Kingdom* [GC], paragraph 120; *Brosset-Triboulet and Others v. France* [GC], paragraph 86; *Depalle v. France* [GC], paragraph 83.
113. *Brosset-Triboulet and Others v. France* [GC], paragraph 87; *Depalle v. France* [GC], paragraph 84.

54. In the case of *Fredin v. Sweden*, the Court considered a restriction on the use of property justified. This case concerned the revocation of a licence to operate a gravel pit situated on the applicants' land on the basis of the Nature Conservation Act. The Court found that the revocation of the licence interfered with the applicants' peaceful enjoyment of their property. However, it also held that it had a legal basis and served the general interest in protecting the environment. The Court underlined that the applicants were aware of the possibility which the authorities had of revoking their licence. While the authorities were under an obligation to take into account their interests when examining whether the licence should be renewed, which they were to do every ten years, this could not have founded any legitimate expectation on the applicants' part of being able to continue exploitation for a long period of time. In addition, the applicants were granted a three-year closing-down period, which was subsequently extended by eleven months at their request. The Court concluded that the revocation was not disproportionate to the legitimate aim pursued, i.e. the protection of the environment, and therefore that Article 1 of Protocol No. 1 was not violated.

55. The *Pine Valley Developments Ltd and Others v. Ireland* judgment and the *Kapsalis and Nima-Kapsali v. Greece*[114] decision both concerned the withdrawal of permissions to build on land purchased for construction. In both cases the Court found that these decisions amounted to a control of the use of property, but that it was lawful in domestic law and that the aim of environmental protection which had been pursued by the authorities when deciding on the withdrawal was both legitimate and in accordance with the general interest. In the *Pine Valley Developments Ltd and Others v. Ireland* case, the interference was aimed at securing the correct application of the planning/environmental legislation not only in the applicants' case but for everyone else. The prevention of building was a proper way of serving the aim of the legislation at issue which was to preserve the green-belt. Moreover, the applicants were engaged in a commercial venture which, by its very nature, involved an element of risk and they were aware not only of the zoning plan but also that the local authorities would oppose any departure from it. The Court concluded that the annulment of the building permission could not be considered disproportionate to the legitimate aim of preservation of

---

114. *Kapsalis and Nima-Kapsali v. Greece*, decision of 23 September 2004.

the environment and thus that there was no violation of Article 1 of Protocol No. 1.[115] In the *Kapsalis and Nima-Kapsali v. Greece* case, the Court held that in fields such as urban planning or the environment, the assessment of the national authorities should prevail unless it is manifestly unreasonable.[116] In the case at hand, the withdrawal of the planning permission was validated by the Administrative High Court following a thorough examination of all aspects of the problem and there was no indication that its decision had been either arbitrary or unforeseeable. Indeed two other building permissions on land situated in the same area as the applicants' own plot had already been annulled by the courts prior to the annulment of the applicants' own permission. Moreover, the decision to allow building in the zone where the applicants' plot was situated had not been finalised when they had purchased it; the authorities could not be blamed for the applicants' negligence in verifying the status of the plot which they were buying. Therefore, the Court considered that the withdrawal of the planning permission was not disproportionate to the aim of protection of the environment and as a result concluded that the complaint should be dismissed as being manifestly ill-founded.

56. The case of *Hamer v. Belgium*[117] related to the demolition of a holiday home, built in 1967 by the applicant's parents without a building permit. In 1994, the police had drawn up two reports: one concerning the cutting of trees on the property in breach of forestry regulations and the other on the construction without a permit of a house in an area of forest for which no permit could have been granted. The applicant had been ordered to restore the site to its original state. The Court acknowledged that the authorities had interfered with the applicant's right to respect for her property under Article 1 of Protocol No. 1, which, however, could be justified in the present case.

57. As to the proportionality of the impugned measure, the Court pointed out that the environment was an asset whose protection was a matter of considerable and constant concern to the public and hence to the authorities. Economic imperatives and even some fundamental rights such as the right to property should not be given precedence over environmental protection, particularly if the state had adopted

---

115. *Pine Valley Developments Ltd and Others v. Ireland*, paragraphs 57-59.
116. *Kapsalis and Nima-Kapsali v. Greece*, paragraph 3, "law" part.
117. *Hamer v. Belgium*, judgment of 27 November 2007 (in French only).

legislation on the subject. As a result, the authorities had a responsibility, which should be translated into action at the appropriate time so as not to divest the environmental protection measures they had decided to implement of any useful effect. Thus, restrictions on the right to property could be permitted provided that a fair balance was struck between the collective and individual interests at stake.[118]

58. Furthermore, the impugned measure had pursued the legitimate aim of protecting an area of forest in which building was prohibited, but what the Court had to decide was whether the advantage deriving from the proper development of the land and the protected forest area where the house was situated could be regarded as proportionate to the inconvenience caused.[119] In this connection, the Court noted that the owners of the holiday home had been in undisturbed and uninterrupted possession of it for a total of thirty-seven years and the authorities, who had known, or should have known, about the existence of the house for a long time, had failed to take the requisite measures and had hence helped to perpetuate a situation which could only undermine efforts to protect the forested area in question. Furthermore, no measure other than complete restoration seemed appropriate given the irrefutable damage that had been done to an area of forest in which building was prohibited. Moreover, in contrast with other cases in which the authorities had been found to have given their implicit consent,[120] this house had been built without permission. Consequently, the Court found that the applicant had not undergone a disproportionate infringement of her right to property and hence that there had been no violation of Article 1 of Protocol No. 1.

59. In the similar case of *Turgut and Others v. Turkey*,[121] the domestic courts had decided to register a piece of land for which the applicants had held a title deed for at least three generations in the name of the Treasury on the ground that the land was public forest. The decision to annul their title to property without compensation was, in the applicants' view, a disproportionate infringement of their right to

---

118. *Hamer v. Belgium*, paragraphs 79-80.
119. *Hamer v. Belgium*, paragraphs 81-82.
120. The cases of the "Turkish coast". See, for example, *N.A. and Others v. Turkey*, judgment of 11 October 2005.
121. *Turgut and Others v. Turkey*, judgment of 8 July 2008 (in French only).

respect for their property. The Court applied the same reasoning as in the Hamer case cited above, taking the view that the purpose of dispossessing the applicants, namely to protect nature and forests, fell within the scope of the public interest referred to in the second sentence of the first paragraph of Article 1 of Protocol No. 1,[122] and that protecting nature and forests and, more generally speaking, the environment was a valuable activity.[123] The Court found, nonetheless, that there had been a violation of Article 1 of Protocol No. 1 because the failure to compensate the applicants rendered the deprivation of property an excessive infringement. This reason was reaffirmed in *Satir v. Turkey* which equally dealt with the question of land expropriation without compensation.[124]

60. Nevertheless, in contrast to the above two more recent Grand Chamber judgments of *Depalle v. France* and *Brosset-Triboulet and Others v. France*[125] underline that even massive infringements on the right to property can be justified through environmental protection. In both cases the Court did not find a violation of Article 1 of Protocol No. 1. Both cases concerned an order for the applicants to demolish their homes that had been built on the seashore in an area of maritime public property where there was no formal right of property or right of temporary occupancy. It had been only by virtue of successive *ad hoc* decisions that the owners had been authorised, over half a century before, to occupy the dyke on the shoreline and to build houses temporarily, and none of these decisions had explicitly had the effect of recognising any property right over the state-owned public property.[126] The authorities ordered the applicants to restore the site to its original state "by demolishing the constructions built on the public property", at their own cost and without compensation. Their decision was taken in the context of a desire to implement an active policy of environmental protection. Hence, the role of the Court was to ensure that a "fair balance" was achieved between the demands of the general interest of the community (environmental protection, free access to

---

122. See, mutatis mutandis, *Lazaridi v. Greece*, judgment of 13 July 2006 (in French only), paragraph 34 and *Şakir Tuğrul Ansay and Others v. Turkey*, Decision of inadmissibility of 2 March 2006 (in French only).
123. *Turgut v. Turkey*, paragraph 90.
124. *Satir v. Turkey*, judgment of 10 March 2009 (French only), paragraphs 33-35.
125. *Depalle v. France* [GC] and *Brosset-Triboulet and Others v. France* [GC], judgments of 29 March 2010.
126. *Depalle v. France*, paragraph 86.

the shore) and those of the applicants, who wanted to keep their houses. In determining whether this requirement was met, the Court recognised that the State enjoyed a wide discretion in its decision-making, particularly in a case like the present one, concerning regional planning and environmental conservation policies where the community's general interest was pre-eminent.[127]

61. The Court held that the applicants could not justifiably claim that the authorities' responsibility for the uncertainty regarding the status of their houses had increased with the passage of time. On the contrary, they had always known that the decisions authorising occupation of the public property were precarious and revocable. The tolerance shown towards them by the State did not alter that fact.[128]

62. It went without saying that after such a long period of time demolition would amount to a radical interference with the applicants' "possessions".[129] However, this was part and parcel of a consistent and rigorous application of the law given the growing need to protect coastal areas and their use by the public, and also to ensure compliance with planning regulations.[130] The Court added lastly that the lack of compensation could not be regarded as a disproportionate measure used to control the use of the applicants' properties, carried out in pursuit of the general interest. The principle that no compensation was payable, which originated in the rules governing public property, had been clearly stated in every decision authorising temporary occupancy of the public property issued to the applicants over decades.[131]

63. Having regard to all the foregoing considerations, the Court held that the applicants would not bear an individual and excessive burden in the event of demolition of their houses without compensation. Accordingly, the balance between the interests of the community and those of the applicants would not be upset. The Court considered that there had not been a violation of Article 1 of Protocol No. 1.

---

127. *Depalle v. France* [GC], paragraphs 83-84 ; *Brosset-Triboulet and Others v. France* [GC], paragraphs 84 and 86-87.
128. *Depalle v. France* [GC], paragraph 86; *Brosset-Triboulet and Others v. France* [GC], paragraph 89.
129. *Depalle v. France* [GC], paragraph 88; *Brosset-Triboulet and Others v. France* [GC], paragraph 92.
130. *Depalle v. France* [GC], paragraphs 81 and 89.
131. *Depalle v. France* [GC], paragraph 91; *Brosset-Triboulet and Others v. France* [GC], paragraph 94.

64. The case of *Valico S. R. L. v. Italy*[132] related to a decision by the national authorities to impose a fine on a company for not complying with rules on the construction of buildings designed to protect the landscape and the environment. The Court examined the complaint under Article 1 of Protocol No. 1 and found that the disputed measure was prescribed by law and pursued the legitimate aim of protecting the landscape and developing the land rationally and in a manner showing due regard for the environment, all of which was in accordance with the general interest. As to the balance between the demands of the general interest and the need to protect the applicant company's fundamental rights, the Court found that even if the impugned change of the construction location, which had not been authorised by the authorities, had not damaged the environment, the simple fact of failing to satisfy the conditions imposed by the authorities responsible for spatial planning and development had constituted a breach of the relevant domestic legal regulations. Furthermore, while the penalty imposed on the applicant company might at first seem excessive, the change in the location of the building had substantially altered the original plans. This was also a large-scale project and the severity of the deterrent penalty had to be in keeping with the importance of the issues at stake. Lastly, there had been no order to demolish the building in question. In view of all of the foregoings, the Court found that the Italian authorities had struck the right balance between the general interest on the one hand and respect for the applicant company's right to property on the other. Accordingly, it considered that the interference had not imposed an excessive burden such as to make it disproportionate to the legitimate aim pursued, and dismissed the applicant's complaint.

65. In another case *Papastavrou and Others v. Greece*[133] the applicants and the authorities were in dispute over the ownership of a plot of land. Following a decision of the prefect, it was decided that the area where the disputed plot was located should be reforested. The applicants unsuccessfully challenged this decision before domestic courts and therefore brought their case before the European Court of Human Rights. They argued that the prefect's decision had not been taken in accordance with the public interest, alleging that the geological characteristics of that area made it unfit for reforestation.

---

132. *Valico S. R. L. v. Italy*, decision of 21 March 2006 (in French only).
133. *Papastavrou and Others v. Greece*, judgment of 10 April 2003, paragraphs 22-39.

The Court recognised the complexity of the issue and the fact that the prefect's decision was based solely on a decision of the Minister of Agriculture made some 60 years earlier, without any fresh reassessment of the situation. It also noted that there was no possibility of obtaining compensation under Greek law. The Court thus concluded that the public authorities had not struck a fair balance between the public interest and the applicants' rights. Accordingly, there had been a violation of Article 1 of Protocol No. 1.

66. In the case of *Z.A.N.T.E. – Marathonisi A.E. v. Greece*,[134] which concerned the compensation in connection with a dispute relating to a small islet which the applicant company had purchased, the Court pointed to the wide margin of appreciation that States were granted when implementing spatial planning policies and held that the interference with the applicant company's right to its property satisfied the requirement of being in the general interest. However, on the matter of compensation, the authorities had argued wrongly that:

it was impossible for the prohibition of building on the disputed land to infringe the right to protection of property as construction on the land in question was, at all events and by its very nature, impossible.

The Court inferred from this that the authorities had applied an irrefutable presumption which took no account of the distinctive features of each piece of land not covered by an urban zone and found that the lack of compensation would give rise to a violation of Article 1 of Protocol No. 1.[135]

(c) On the other hand, protection of the individual right to the peaceful enjoyment of one's possessions may require the public authorities to ensure certain environmental standards. The effective exercise of this right does not depend merely on the public authorities' duty not to interfere, but may require them to take positive measures to protect this right, particularly where there is a direct link between the measures an applicant may legitimately expect from the authorities and his

---

134. *Z.A.N.T.E. – Marathonisi A.E. v. Greece, judgment of* 7 December 2007 (in French only).
135. *Z.A.N.T.E. – Marathonisi A.E. v. Greece*, paragraphs 50-52.

or her effective enjoyment of his or her possessions.[136] The Court has found that such an obligation may arise in respect of dangerous activities and to a lesser extent in situations of natural disasters.[137]

67. Pursuant to the Court's interpretation of Article 1 of Protocol No. 1, in certain circumstances, public authorities must not only refrain from directly infringing the right to protection of property, but they may also be required to take active steps to ensure that this right is respected in practice. In the context of dangerous activities where the right of property is at risk, public authorities may therefore be expected to take measures to ensure that this right is not breached.

68. In *Öneryıldız v. Turkey*,[138] the applicant's home was destroyed by an explosion which took place on the rubbish tip next to where his family's house had been built illegally. The Court noted that the authorities had tolerated its existence for a number of years. It considered therefore that the applicant could claim protection from Article 1 of Protocol No. 1 despite the fact that his dwelling had been illegally built. The Court also found that there was a causal link between the gross negligence attributable to the authorities and the destruction of the applicant's house. Because the Court considered that the treatment of waste, as a matter relating to industrial development and urban planning, is regulated and controlled by the State, it brought the accidents in this sphere within the State's responsibility. Therefore, the authorities were required to do everything within their power to protect private proprietary interests. Consequently, finding that certain suitable preventive measures existed, which the national authorities could have taken to avert the environmental risk, that had been brought to their attention, the Court concluded that the national authorities' failure to take the necessary measures amounted to a breach of their positive obligation under Article 1 of Protocol No. 1.

69. Similarly in the case of *Budayeva and Others v. Russia*,[139] the Court needed to consider to what extent the authorities were expected to take measures to protect property from natural disasters. However, the Court distinguished that:

---

136. *Öneryıldız v. Turkey* [GC], paragraph 134; *Budayeva and Others v. Russia*, judgment of 22 March 2008, paragraph 172.

137. *Öneryıldız v. Turkey* [GC], paragraphs 134 and 135; *Budayeva and Others v. Russia*, paragraphs 172-182.

138. For a short description of the case, see paragraph 4 of the manual.

139. *Budayeva and Others v. Russia*, judgment of 22 March 2008.

natural disasters, which are as such beyond human control, do not call for the same extent of State involvement. Accordingly, its positive obligations as regards the protection of property from weather hazards do not extend necessarily as far as in the sphere of dangerous activities of a man-made nature.

The latter require national authorities to do everything in their power to protect lives.[140] Differentiating between the positive obligations under Article 2 of the Convention and those under Article 1 of Protocol No. 1 to the Convention the Court went on to state:

While the fundamental importance of the right to life requires that the scope of the positive obligations under Article 2 includes a duty to do everything within the authorities' power in the sphere of disaster relief for the protection of that right, the obligation to protect the right to the peaceful enjoyment of possessions, which is not absolute, cannot extend further than what is reasonable in the circumstances. Accordingly, the authorities enjoy a wider margin of appreciation in deciding what measures to take in order to protect individuals' possessions from weather hazards than in deciding on the measures needed to protect lives.[141]

In this case the Court noted that the mudslide had been exceptionally powerful and that there had been no clear causal link between the State's failure to take measures and the extent of the physical damage. It also observed that the damage could not be unequivocally attributed in its entirety to State negligence as the alleged negligence had been no more than an aggravating factor contributing to the damage caused by natural forces. Moreover, it held that the procedural duty with regard to an independent inquiry or judicial response is also not comprehensive compared to Article 2.[142] Additionally, the Court considered that "the positive obligation on the State to protect private property from natural disaster cannot be construed as binding the State to compensate the full market value of destroyed property."[143] Consequently, it found that there had been no violation of Article 1 of Protocol No. 1.

---

140. *Budayeva and Others v. Russia*, paragraph 174.
141. *Budayeva and Others v. Russia*, paragraph 175.
142. *Budayeva and Others v. Russia*, paragraphs 176, 178 and 182.
143. *Budayeva and Others v. Russia*, paragraph 182.

Chapter IV: Information
and communication
on environmental matters

ARTICLE 10
FREEDOM OF EXPRESSION

1. Everyone has the right to freedom of expression. This right shall include freedom to hold opinions and to receive and impart information and ideas without interference by public authority and regardless of frontiers. [...]

2. The exercise of these freedoms, since it carries with it duties and responsibilities, may be subject to such formalities, conditions, restrictions or penalties as are prescribed by law and are necessary in a democratic society, in the interests of national security, territorial integrity or public safety, for the prevention of disorder or crime, for the protection of health or morals, for the protection of the reputation or rights of others, for preventing the disclosure of information received in confidence, or for maintaining the authority and impartiality of the judiciary.

Right to receive and impart information and ideas on environmental matters

(a) The right to receive and impart information and ideas is guaranteed by Article 10 of the Convention. In the particular context of the environment, the Court has found that there exists a strong public interest in enabling individuals and groups to contribute to the public debate by disseminating information and ideas on matters of general public interest.[144]

70. Freedom of expression is a cornerstone of democracy. It enables debate and the free exchange of ideas. The right to distribute information on environmental matters can be seen as just one example of the rights that Article 10 seeks to protect. Clearly, this right protects individuals from direct actions of the public authorities, such as censorship. However, this right may also be relevant when a private party takes legal action against another private party to stop the distribution of information.

71. The issue of the right of environmental activists to distribute material was raised in *Steel and Morris v. the United Kingdom*. This case involved two environmental activists who were associated with a campaign against McDonald's. As part of that campaign, a leaflet called "What's wrong with McDonald's?" was produced and distributed. McDonald's sued the two applicants for libel. The trial lasted 313 days and the applicants did not receive any legal aid even though they were unemployed or earning low wages at the time. McDonald's won substantial damages against them. The European Court of Human Rights recognised that large multinational companies like McDonald's had the right to defend their reputation in court proceedings but stressed at the same time that small and informal campaign groups had to be able to carry on their activities effectively. The Court considered it essential, in the interests of open debate, that in court proceedings involving both big companies and small campaign groups there is fairness and equality of arms between them. Otherwise, there might be a possible "chilling effect" on the general interest in promoting the free circulation of information and

144. *Steel and Morris v. the United Kingdom*, judgment of 15 February 2005, paragraph 89; *Vides Aizsardzības Klubs v. Latvia*, judgment of 27 May 2004, paragraph 40.

ideas about the activities of powerful commercial entities. By not granting legal aid to the applicants, the United Kingdom had not guaranteed fairness in the court proceedings. This lack of fairness and the substantial damages awarded against them meant, according to the Court, that the applicants' freedom of expression had been violated.

(b) Restrictions by public authorities on the right to receive and impart information and ideas, including on environmental matters, must be prescribed by law and follow a legitimate aim. Measures interfering with this right must be proportionate to the legitimate aim pursued and a fair balance must therefore be struck between the interest of the individual and the interest of the community as a whole.[145]

72. As is clear from the text of paragraph 2 of Article 10, freedom of expression is not an absolute right. However, when public authorities take steps which may interfere with freedom of expression, their actions must fulfil three requirements. These are cumulative, meaning all three must be present for the restriction to be permitted under Article 10. Firstly, there must be a legal basis for their action and the relevant domestic law must be accessible and its effects foreseeable. Secondly, their action must pursue one of the interests set out in Article 10 paragraph 2. Finally, their action must be necessary in a democratic society. This third requirement implies that the means used by the authorities must be proportionate to the interest pursued. The Court has frequently stated that the adjective "necessary" in paragraph 2 implies the existence of a "pressing social need".[146] The level of protection ultimately given to the expression in question will depend on the particular circumstances of the case including the nature of the restriction, the degree of interference and the type of information or opinions concerned.

73. Given that the information that environmental groups or activists will want to distribute is often of a sensitive nature, the level of protection will as a rule be high. By way of an example, in *Vides Aizsardzības Klubs v. Latvia*, the applicant was an environmental

---

145. *Vides Aizsardzības Klubs v. Latvia*, paragraph 40.
146. E.g. *The Observer and Guardian v. the United Kingdom*, judgment of 26 November 1991, paragraph 59.

association which alleged that a local mayor had not halted building works which were causing damage to the coastline. The mayor sued the association. The Latvian court found that the association had not proven its allegations and ordered it to publish an apology and pay damages to the mayor. The European Court of Human Rights noted that the association had been trying to draw attention to a sensitive issue. As a non-governmental organisation specialised in the relevant area, the applicant organisation had been exercising its role of a public "watchdog". That kind of participation by association was essential in a democratic society. In the Court's view, the applicant organisation had expressed a personal view of the law amounting to a value judgement. It could not therefore be required to prove the accuracy of that assessment. The Court held that, in a democratic society, the public authorities were, as a rule, exposed to permanent scrutiny by citizens and, subject to acting in good faith, everyone should be able to draw the public's attention to situations that they considered unlawful. As a result, despite the discretion afforded to the national authorities, the Court held that there had not been a reasonable relationship of proportionality between the restrictions imposed on the freedom of expression of the applicant organisation and the legitimate aim pursued. The Court therefore concluded that there had been a violation of Article 10.

74. In the cases of *Verein gegen Tierfabriken v. Switzerland*[147] the Court had to consider whether the national authorities' refusal to register an advertisement of an animal protection association fulfilled the requirement of Article 10. The applicant association had made a television commercial in response to various advertisements produced by the meat industry, which showed, *inter alia*, a noisy hall with pigs in small pens, gnawing nervously at the iron bars. The voiceover compared the conditions in which pigs were reared to concentration camps, and added that the animals were pumped full of medicines. The film concluded with the exhortation: "Eat less meat, for the sake of your health, the animals and the environment!" The Court held that the refusal to register an advertisement that was necessary to be aired in Switzerland amounted to interference and continued to assess whether the interference might be justified

---

147. *Verein gegen Tierfabriken v. Switzerland*, judgment of 28 June 2001; *Verein gegen Tierfabriken v. Switzerland*, judgment of 4 October 2007; *Verein gegen Tierfabriken v. Switzerland* (No. 2), judgment of 30 June 2009.

through the condition set out in paragraph 2 of Article 10. It analysed whether it was prescribed by law, motivated by legitimate aims and was necessary in a democratic society.[148] Thereby the law must be sufficiently precise, accessible and its consequences must be foreseeable.[149] The Court underlined that the phrase "necessary in a democratic society" requires a "pressing social need".[150] The Court held that, because the content of the advertisement was not commercial but "political" and it pertained to the general European debate on the protection of animals and the manner in which they are reared, the extent of the margin of appreciation of whether public authorities can ban the advertisement is reduced. This is because it is not a given individual's purely commercial interests that are at stake, but the participation in a debate affecting the general interest.[151] In consequence, the Court considered the ban disproportionate.

(c) Freedom to receive information under Article 10 can neither be construed as imposing on public authorities a general obligation to collect and disseminate information relating to the environment of their own motion.

75. In *Guerra and Others v. Italy*,[152] the applicants complained – among other things – that the authorities' failure to inform the public about the hazards of the factory and about the procedures to be followed in the event of a major accident, infringed their right to freedom of information as guaranteed by Article 10. However, the Court found that no obligation on States to collect, process and disseminate environmental information of their own motion could be derived from Article 10. Such an obligation would prove hard for public authorities to implement by reason of the difficulty for them to determine among other things how and when the information should be disclosed and who should be receiving it.[153] However, freedom to receive information under Article 10 as interpreted by the Court

---

148. *Verein gegen Tierfabriken v. Switzerland*, judgment of 28 June 2001, paragraphs 48-49.
149. *Verein gegen Tierfabriken v. Switzerland*, paragraphs 55-57.
150. *Verein gegen Tierfabriken v. Switzerland*, paragraph 67.
151. *Verein gegen Tierfabriken v. Switzerland*, paragraphs 70-71.
152. For a short description of the case, see paragraph 30 of the manual.
153. *Guerra and Others v. Italy* [GC], paragraph 51.

prohibits public authorities from restricting a person from receiving information that others wish or may be willing to impart to him or her.

Access to information on environmental matters

(d) However, Articles 2 and 8 of the Convention may impose a specific positive obligation on public authorities to ensure a right of access to information in relation to environmental issues in certain circumstances.[154]

(e) This obligation to *ensure access to information* is generally complemented by the positive obligations of the public authorities to *provide information* to those persons whose right to life under Article 2 or whose right to respect for private and family life and the home under Article 8 are threatened. The Court has found that in the particular context of dangerous activities falling within the responsibility of the State, special emphasis should be placed on the public's right to information.[155] Additionally, the Court held that States are duty-bound based on Article 2 to "adequately inform the public about any life threatening emergencies, including natural disasters".[156]

76. As mentioned under the previous principle, the Court stated in the *Guerra and Others v. Italy* case[157] that Article 10 was not applicable because this article basically prohibits public authorities from restricting a person from receiving information that others wish or may be willing to impart to him or her. The Court did find in this case, however, that Article 8 had been violated by the failure to make information available which would have enabled the applicants to assess the risks they and their families might run if they continued to live near the factory.[158]

---

154. *Öneryıldız v. Turkey* [GC], paragraph 90; *Guerra and Others v. Italy* [GC], paragraph 60.
155. *Öneryıldız v. Turkey* [GC], paragraph 90.
156. *Budayeva and Others v. Russia*, judgment of 22 March 2008 paragraph 131.
157. For a short description of the case, see paragraph 30 of the manual.
158. *Guerra and Others v. Italy* [GC], paragraph 60.

77. Likewise in *Tătar v. Romania*, a case in which the authorities had prolonged the operation permit of a gold mine that did not fulfil all required health and environmental standards, the Court examined whether the national authorities had adequately informed the villagers of nearby settlements about potential health risks and environmental impact.[159]

78. As to the right to information in circumstances where life is at risk, the Court considered in *Öneryıldız v. Turkey*[160] that similar requirements arose under Article 2 as those it had found were applicable under Article 8 in the Guerra and Others case, and that in this context particular emphasis had to be placed on the public's right to information. Importantly, the Court sharpened the scope of the duty to inform derived from *Guerra and Others v. Italy*. The Court found a duty to inform exists in situation of "real and imminent dangers" either to the applicants' physical integrity or the sphere of their private lives. The Court held that the fact that the applicant was in the position to assess some of the risks, in particular health risks, does not absolve the public authorities from their duty to proactively inform the applicant. Therefore the Court found that there was a violation of Article 2. The Court concluded in the present case that the administrative authorities knew or ought to have known that the inhabitants of certain slum areas were faced with a real and immediate risk both to their physical integrity and their lives on account of the deficiencies of the municipal rubbish tip. In addition to not remedying the situation, the authorities failed to comply with their duty to inform the inhabitants of this area of potential health and environmental risks, which might have enabled the applicant to assess the serious dangers for himself and his family without diverting State resources to an unrealistic degree. However, the Court also found that even if public authorities respect the right of information this may not be sufficient to absolve the State of its responsibilities under Article 2, unless more practical measures are also taken to avoid the risks.

79. The Court reaffirmed this position in *Budayeva and Others v. Russia*.[161] However, it added that the obligation on the part of the State to safeguard the lives of those within its jurisdiction includes

---

159. *Tătar v. Romania*, judgment of 27 January 2009, paragraphs 101 and 113.
160. For a short description of the case, see paragraph 4 of the manual. *Öneryıldız v. Turkey* [GC], paragraphs 67 and 84-87.
161. *Budayeva and Others v. Russia*, paragraphs 131-132.

substantive and procedural aspects, which *inter alia*, contains a positive obligation to not only take regulatory measures and to ensure that any occasion of death during life-threatening emergencies is adequately investigated, but also to adequately inform the public about any life-threatening emergencies. In this case the authorities had failed to share information about the possibility of mudslides with the population. This was reaffirmed in *Brânduşe v. Romania.*[162]

(f) Access to information is of importance to individuals because it can allay their fears and enables them to assess the environmental danger to which they may be exposed.

80. In *McGinley and Egan v. the United Kingdom*, the applicants were soldiers in the Pacific when the British Government carried out nuclear tests there. They argued that non-disclosure of records relating to those tests violated their rights under Article 8 because the records would have enabled them to determine whether or not they had been exposed to dangerous levels of radiation, so that they could assess the possible consequences of the tests to their health. The Court found that Article 8 was applicable on the ground that the issue of access to information which could either have allayed the applicants' fears or enabled them to assess the danger to which they had been exposed was sufficiently closely linked to their private and family lives to raise an issue under Article 8. It further held that where a government engages in hazardous activities which might have hidden adverse consequences on human health, respect for private and family life under Article 8 requires that an effective and accessible procedure be established which enables persons involved in such activities to seek all relevant and appropriate information. If there is an obligation of disclosure, individuals must not be required to obtain it through lengthy and complex litigation.[163] In the instant case, however, the Court found that the applicants had not taken the necessary steps to request certain documents which could have informed them about the radiation levels in the areas in which they were stationed during the tests, and which might have served to reassure them in this respect. The Court concluded that by providing a procedure for requesting documents the state had fulfilled its positive obligation under Article 8 and that therefore there had been no violation of this provision.

---

162. *Brânduşe v. Romania*, judgment of 7 April 2009 (available in French only), paragraph 63.
163. *Roche v. the United Kingdom* [GC], judgment 19 October 2005, paragraph 165.

81. In the *Guerra and Others v. Italy* case, the Court explicitly noted that the applicants had not had access to essential information that would have enabled them to assess the risks that they and their families might run if they continued to live in a town particularly exposed to danger in the event of an accident at a factory located nearby. The Court concluded that the Italian authorities had failed to guarantee the applicants' rights under Article 8 for not having communicated relevant information on the dangers of the factory. More generally, the Court has emphasised the importance of public access to the conclusions of studies and to information which would enable members of the public to assess the danger to which they are exposed.[164] The Court held likewise in *Giacomelli v. Italy,*[165] *Tătar v. Romania,*[166] and *Lemke v. Turkey.*[167]

(g) Moreover, the Court has established criteria on the construction of the procedures used to provide information. It held that when public authorities engage in dangerous activities which they know involve adverse risks to health, they must establish an effective and accessible procedure to enable individuals to seek all relevant and appropriate information.[168] Moreover, if environmental and health impact assessments are carried out, the public needs to have access to those study results.[169]

82. In the *Brânduşe v. Romania* case, the Court noted that the government had not stated what measures had been taken by the authorities to ensure that the inmates in the local prison, including the applicant, who had asked for information about the disputed rubbish tip in close proximity of the prison facility, would have proper access to the conclusions of environmental studies and information by means of which the health risks to which they were exposed could be assessed.[170] Consequently, the Court found that there was a violation of Article 8 based partially on the authorities' failure to secure the applicant's right to access to information.

---

164. *Taşkın and Others v. Turkey,* paragraph 119.
165. *Giacomelli v. Italy,* judgment of 2 November 2006, paragraph 83.
166. *Tătar v. Romania,* paragraph 113.
167. *Lemke v. France,* paragraph 41.
168. *McGinley and Egan v. the United Kingdom,* judgment of 9 June 1998, paragraphs 97 and 101.
169. *Brânduşe v. Romania,* judgment of 7 April 2009, paragraph 63.
170. *Brânduşe v. Romania,* paragraphs 63 and 74. Similarly *Guerra and Others v. Italy* [GC], paragraph 60.

83. Similarly, in the case of *Giacomelli v. Italy*,[171] which concerned a waste treatment factory, but also in *Lemke v. Turkey*,[172] which concerned the operation of a gold mine, the Court pointed out that

a governmental decision-making process concerning complex issues of environmental and economic policy must in the first place involve appropriate investigations and studies [...]. The importance of public access to the conclusions of such studies and to information enabling members of the public to assess the danger to which they are exposed is beyond question (see, mutatis mutandis, Guerra and Others, cited above, paragraph 60, and McGinley and Egan v. the United Kingdom, judgment of 9 June 1998).[173]

84. This conviction was also echoed in the case of *Tătar v. Romania*,[174] where the Court had to decide whether the prolonged authorisation of the operation of gold mine complied with the authorities' obligations resulting from Article 8. With regard to the right to access to information, the Court noted that the national legislation on public debates had not been complied with as the participants in those debates had not had access to the conclusions of the study on which the contested decision to grant the company authorisation to operate was based. Interestingly, in this case, the Court referred once more to international environmental standards. It pointed out that the rights of access to information, public participation in decision-making and access to justice in environmental matters were enshrined in the Aarhus Convention[175] and that one of the effects of the Council of Europe's Parliamentary Assembly Resolution 1430 (2005) on industrial hazards was to extend the duty of States to improve dissemination of information in this sphere.[176]

---

171. *Giacomelli v. Italy*, judgment of 2 November 2006, paragraph 83. For a short description of the case, see paragraph 41 of the manual.
172. *Lemke v. Turkey*, judgment of 5 June 2007. For a short description of the case, see paragraph 43 of the manual.
173. *Giacomelli v. Italy*, paragraph 83 and *Lemke v. Turkey*, paragraph 41.
174. *Tătar v. Romania*, judgment of 27 January 2009.
175. Convention on Access to Information, Public Participation in Decision-making and Access to Justice in Environmental Matters, adopted on 25 June 1998 in Aarhus, Denmark.
176. *Tătar v. Romania*, paragraphs 93, 101, 113-116 and 118.

Chapter V: Decision-making processes in environmental matters and public participation in them

(a) When making decisions which relate to the environment, public authorities must take into account the interests of individuals who may be affected.[177] In this context, it is important that the public is able to make representations to the public authorities.[178]

(b) Where public authorities have complex issues of environmental and economic policy to determine,[179] the decision-making process must involve appropriate investigations and studies in order to predict and evaluate in advance the effects on the environment and to enable them to strike a fair balance between the various conflicting interests at stake.[180] The Court has stressed the importance of public access to the conclusions of such studies and to information which would enable individuals to assess the danger to which they are exposed.[181] However, this does not mean that decisions can be taken only if comprehensive and measurable data are available in relation to each and every aspect of the matter to be decided.[182]

85. The Court has recognised the importance of ensuring that individuals are involved in the decision-making processes leading to decisions which could affect the environment and where their rights under the Convention are at stake.

86. In *Hatton and Others v. the United Kingdom,*[183] for instance, which related to the noise[184] generated by aircraft taking off and landing at an international airport and the regulatory regime governing it, the Court examined the question of public participation in the decision-making process in the context of Article 8 considering that it had a bearing on the quiet enjoyment of the applicants' private and family life and home. It deemed that in cases involving decisions by public

---

177. *Hatton and Others v. the United Kingdom* [GC], judgment of 8 July 2003, paragraph 99; *Chapman v. the United Kingdom* [GC], judgment of 18 January 2001, paragraph 92.

178. *Hatton and Others v. the United Kingdom* [GC], paragraph 128.

179. *Hatton and Others v. the United Kingdom* [GC], paragraph 128; *Taşkın and Others v. Turkey,* judgment of 10 November 2004, paragraph 119.

180. *Hatton and Others v. the United Kingdom* [GC], paragraph 128; *Taşkın and Others v. Turkey,* 2004, paragraph 119.

181. *Taşkın and Others v. Turkey,* paragraph 119.

182. *Hatton and Others v. the United Kingdom* [GC], paragraphs 104 and 128; *G. and E. v. Norway,* admissibility decision of 3 October 1983; *Giacomelli v. Italy,* judgment of 2 November 2007, paragraph 82.

183. For a short description of the case, see paragraph 28 of the manual.

184. *Taşkın and Others v. Turkey,* paragraph 119.

authorities which affect environmental issues, there are two aspects to the inquiry which may be carried out by the Court. First, the Court may assess the substantive merits of the government's decision, to ensure that it is compatible with Article 8. Secondly, it may scrutinise the decision-making process to ensure that due weight has been accorded to the interests of the individual. This means that in such cases the Court is required to consider all procedural aspects of the process leading to the decision in question, including the type of policy or decision involved, the extent to which the views of individuals were taken into account throughout the decision-making procedure and the procedural safeguards available, i.e. whether the individuals concerned could challenge the decision before the courts or some other independent body, if they believed that their interests and representations had not been properly taken into account.

87. The Court concluded in the *Hatton and Others v. the United Kingdom* case that there had not been fundamental procedural flaws in the preparation of the scheme on limitations for night flights and, therefore, no violation of Article 8 in this respect, in view of the following elements. The Court noted that the authorities had consistently monitored the situation and that night flights had been restricted as early as 1962. The applicants had access to relevant documentation and it would have been open to them to make representations. If their representations had not been taken into account, it would have been possible for them to challenge subsequent decisions or the scheme itself in court.

88. The principles summarised in *Hatton and Others v. the United Kingdom* have been consistently applied throughout the Court's case-law. They are repeated almost verbatim in numerous judgments, for instance *Giacomelli v. Italy,*[185] *Lemke v. Turkey,*[186] *Tătar v. Romania,*[187] *Taşkın and Others v. Turkey,*[188] *McMichael v. the United Kingdom,*[189] *Brânduşe v. Romania,*[190] *Dubetska and Others v. Ukraine*[191] and *Grimkovskaya v. Ukraine.*[192]

---

185. *Giacomelli v. Italy,* paragraphs 82-84 and 94.
186. *Lemke v. Turkey,* judgment of 5 September 2007, paragraph 41.
187. *Tătar v. Romania,* judgment of 27 January 2009, paragraphs 88, 101 and 113.
188. *Taşkın and Others v. Turkey,* paragraphs 118-119.
189. *McMichael v. the United Kingdom,* judgment of 24 February 1995, paragraph 87, also *McGinley and Egan v. the United Kingdom,* judgment of 9 June 1998, paragraph 97.
190. *Brânduşe v. Romania,* judgment of 7 July 2009, paragraphs 62-63.
191. *Dubetska and Others v. Ukraine,* paragraphs 66-69.
192. *Grimkovskaya v. Ukraine,* paragraphs 66-69.

89. However, considering the facts of the subsequent cases the scope of the required decision-making procedure has become more evident. For example, considering *Giacomelli v. Italy* the Court acknowledges that national authorities have failed to respect the procedural machinery provided for to respect the individual rights in the licensing of a waste treatment plant. In particular, they did not accord any weight to national judicial decisions and did not conduct an "environmental impact assessment" which is necessary for every project with potential harmful environmental consequences as prescribed also by national law.[193]

90. The Court's finding of a violation of Article 8 in *Grimkovskaya v. Ukraine*[194] resulted from the authority's negligence of minimal procedural safeguards which are necessary to strike a fair balance between the applicant's and the community's interest. Firstly, the Court noted that the decision to route the motorway through the city was not preceded by an adequate feasibility study, assessing the probability of compliance with applicable environmental standards and enabling interested parties to contribute their views. It criticised the absence of public access to relevant environmental information. Secondly, the Court required that at the time of taking the routing decision, the authorities should have put in place a reasonable policy for mitigating the motorways effects on the residents. This should have happened not only as the result of repeated complaints by the residents. This did not happen. Lastly, the Court criticised the lack of the ability to challenge the authorities' decision before an independent authority (see Chapter VI below).[195]

91. The Court stressed in *Dubetska and Others v. Ukraine*[196] that it examined whether the authorities conducted sufficient studies to evaluate the risks of a potentially hazardous activity and whether, on the basis of the information available, they have developed an adequate policy vis-à-vis polluters and whether all necessary measures have been taken to enforce this policy in good time. The Court was particularly interested in the extent to which the individuals affected by the policy at issue were able to contribute to the decision-making. This included them having access to the

---

193. *Giacomelli v. Italy,* paragraphs 94-95.
194. For a short description of the case, see paragraph 22 of the manual.
195. *Grimkovskaya v. Ukraine,* paragraphs 66-69.
196. For a short description of the case, see paragraph 21 of the manual.

relevant information and the ability to challenge the authorities' decision in an effective way. Moreover, the Court stated that the procedural safeguards available to the applicant may be rendered inoperative and the state may be found liable under the Convention where a decision-making procedure is unjustifiably lengthy or where a decision taken as a result remains for an important period unenforced.[197]

92. The cases of *Tătar v. Romania*[198] and *Taşkın and Others v. Turkey*[199] explicitly recognise and stress that despite the fact that Article 8 does not contain an explicit procedural requirement, the decision-making process leading to measures of interference must be fair and afford due respect to the interests of the individual as safeguarded by the article.[200] At the same time both cases, which concerned the operation of mines, underlined that only those specifically affected have a right to participate in the decision-making. An *actio popularis* to protect the environment is not envisaged by the Court.[201]

93. Moreover, even though the Court has not yet used the word "environmental impact assessment (EIA)" to describe the procedural aspect of Article 8 – it has only found that states neglected to conduct "EIAs" that were prescribed by national law (see *Giacomelli v. Italy* above) – the Court appears to require more and more EIAs to fulfil the evaluation requirements set out by it. This is supported by the Court's finding in *Tătar v. Romania* which was based partially on the conclusion that the national authorities had failed in their duty to assess, in advance, possible risks of their activities in a satisfactory manner and take adequate measures capable of protecting specifically the right for private and family life and, more generally, the right to the enjoyment of a healthy and protected environment.[202] Overall, the Court is ever more willing to precisely rule on the proper procedures to take environmental matters into account.

---

197. *Dubetska and Others v. Ukraine*, paragraphs 143-144.
198. For a short description of the case, see paragraph 23 of the manual.
199. For a short description of the case, see paragraph 26 of the manual.
200. *Tătar v. Romania*, paragraph 88; *Taşkın and Others v. Turkey*, paragraph 118.
201. The incompatibility of *actio popularis* with the Convention system has been confirmed also in *Ilhan v. Turkey*, judgment of 27 June 2000, paragraphs 52-53.
202. *Tătar v. Romania*, paragraph 112.

Chapter VI: Access to justice and other remedies in environmental matters

ARTICLE 6 PARAGRAPH 1
RIGHT TO A FAIR TRIAL

In the determination of his civil rights and obligations or of any criminal charge against him, everyone is entitled to a fair and public hearing within a reasonable time by an independent and impartial tribunal established by law. Judgment shall be pronounced publicly but the press and public may be excluded from all or part of the trial in the interests of morals, public order or national security in a democratic society, where the interests of juveniles or the protection of the private life of the parties so require, or to the extent strictly necessary in the opinion of the court in special circumstances where publicity would prejudice the interests of justice.

ARTICLE 13
RIGHT TO AN EFFECTIVE REMEDY

Everyone whose rights and freedoms as set forth in this Convention are violated shall have an effective remedy before a national authority notwithstanding that the violation has been committed by persons acting in an official capacity.

(a) Several provisions of the Convention guarantee that individuals should be able to commence judicial or administrative proceedings in order to protect their rights. Article 6 guarantees the right to a fair trial, which the Court has found includes the right of access to a court. Article 13 guarantees to persons, who have an arguable claim that their rights and freedoms as set forth in the Convention have been violated, an effective remedy before a national authority. Moreover, the Court has inferred procedural requirements from certain provisions of the Convention, such as Articles 2 and 8 and Article 1 of Protocol No. 1.[203] All these provisions may apply in cases where human rights and environmental issues are involved.

(b) The right of access to a court under Article 6 will as a rule come into play when a "civil right or obligation", within the meaning of the Convention, is the subject of a "dispute".[204] This includes the right to see final and enforceable court decisions executed and implies that all parties, including public authorities, must respect court decisions.[205]

94. Article 6, guaranteeing the right to a fair trial, is one of the most litigated of all the rights of the Convention. Therefore, a great deal of case-law exists on the requirements of Article 6 paragraph 1 of "a fair and public hearing within a reasonable time by an independent and impartial tribunal established by law". The case-law elaborates a number of other requirements relating to the issue of fairness, including equality of arms which entails that both parties should be given the opportunity to present their cases and adduce evidence under conditions that do not substantially disadvantage one another, and that each party should have the opportunity to comment on the arguments and evidence submitted by the other party. Other requirements also flow from the case-law on the issue of fair trial, for instance that the parties should normally be entitled to appear in person before the courts upon request and that courts should give reasoned decisions.

95. The Court has found that the right of access to a court is also one of the components of the right to a fair trial protected by Article 6. The text of the Convention alone does not contain an express reference to the right of access to a court. However, the case-law of the Court has established that the right of access to court – that is the right to institute proceedings before courts in civil and administrative matters – is an inherent part of the fair trial guarantees provided by

---

203. E.g. *Öneryıldız v. Turkey* [GC], paragraphs 89-96; *Hatton and Others v. the United Kingdom* [GC], paragraph 98.
204. *Balmer-Schafroth and Others v. Switzerland* [GC], judgment of 26 August 1997, paragraph 32; *Athanassoglou and Others v. Switzerland* [GC], judgment of 6 April 2000, paragraph 43.
205. *Kyrtatos v. Greece*, paragraph 32; *Taşkın v. Turkey*, paragraph 134; *Lemke v. Turkey*, judgment 5 June 2007, paragraphs 42 and 52.

Article 6. In one of its early judgments,[206] the Court held that Article 6 "secures to everyone the right to have any claim related to his civil rights and obligations brought before a court or tribunal".

96. In order for Article 6 paragraph 1 to be applicable in civil cases, there must be a "dispute"[207] over a "civil right or obligation". Such a dispute must be genuine and serious. It may be related not only to the actual existence of the right but also to its scope and the manner in which it is exercised.[208] The outcome of the proceedings must be directly decisive for the rights in question. The Court has given the notion of "civil rights and obligations" an autonomous meaning for the purposes of the Convention: whilst it must be a right or an obligation recognised in the national legal system, the Court will not necessarily follow distinctions made in national legal systems between private and public law matters or limit the application of Article 6 to disputes between private parties. The Court has not sought to provide a comprehensive definition of what is meant by a "civil right or obligation" for these purposes.

97. In cases concerning environmental pollution, applicants may invoke their right to have their physical integrity and the enjoyment of their property adequately protected. These rights are recognised in the national law of most European countries and constitute therefore "civil rights" within the meaning of Article 6 paragraph 1.[209] The Court has recognised that an enforceable right to live in a healthy and balanced environment as enshrined in national law constituted a "civil right" within the meaning of Article 6 paragraph 1.[210] In *Zander v. Sweden*, the Court recognised that the protection under Swedish law for landowners against the water in their wells being polluted constituted a "civil right" within the meaning of Article 6 paragraph 1. Since it was not possible for the applicants to have the government's decision reviewed by a court, the Court found a violation of this article. In *Taşkın and Others* and *Öçkan and Others v. Turkey* the Court found Article 6 paragraph 1 applicable as the Turkish Constitution (Article 56) recognised the right to live in a healthy and

---

206. *Golder v. the United Kingdom*, judgment of 21 February 1975, paragraph 36.
207. *"Contestation"* in the French text.
208. *Taşkın and Others v. Turkey*, paragraph 130.
209. See *Balmer-Schafroth and Others v. Switzerland* [GC], paragraph 33; *Athanassoglou and Others v. Switzerland* [GC], paragraph 44; *Taşkın and Others v. Turkey*, paragraph 90.
210. See *Balmer-Schafroth and Others v. Switzerland* [GC], paragraph 33; *Athanassoglou and Others v. Switzerland* [GC], paragraph 44; *Taşkın and Others v. Turkey*, paragraph 90.

balanced environment.[211] In other cases the "rights" of individuals to build on or develop their land, or to protect the pecuniary value of their land by objecting to the development of neighbouring land, have been considered as "civil rights" for the purposes of Article 6.[212]

98. In contrast, Article 6 is not applicable where the right invoked by the applicant is merely a procedural right under administrative law which is not related to the defence of any specific right which he or she may have under domestic law.[213]

99. The right of access to a court which is derived from Article 6 paragraph 1 is not an absolute right. Restrictions may be compatible with the Convention if they have a legitimate purpose and are proportionate to their aim. On the other hand, legal or factual restrictions on this right may be in violation of the Convention if they impede the applicant's effective right of access to a court.

100. In addition, the Court has established that the right to the enforcement of a court decision forms an integral part of the right to a fair trial and of access to a court under Article 6 paragraph 1. The right to institute proceedings before courts would be illusory and deprived of any useful effect if a national legal system allowed a final court decision to remain inoperative.[214] This holds true in cases related to the environment where issues under Article 6 arise. In the *Taşkın and Others v. Turkey* judgment, the Court found a violation under Article 6 paragraph 1 on the ground that the authorities had failed to comply within a reasonable time with an administrative court judgment, later confirmed by the Turkish Supreme Administrative Court, annulling a mining permit by reason of its adverse effects on the environment and human health.[215] In *Kyrtatos v. Greece*,[216] the Court found that by failing for more than seven years to take the necessary measures to comply with two final court decisions quashing building permits on the ground of their

---

211. *Öçkan and Others v. Turkey,* paragraph 52; *Taşkın and Others v. Turkey,* paragraphs 130-134.
212. E.g. *Allan Jacobsson v. Sweden (No. 1),* judgment of 19 February 1998, paragraph 42; *Fredin v. Sweden (No. 1),* judgment of 18 February 1991, paragraph 63; *Ortenberg v. Austria,* judgment of 25 November 1994, paragraph 28.
213. *Ünver v. Turkey,* decision of 26 September 2000, paragraph 2, "law" part.
214. E.g. *Hornsby v. Greece,* judgment of 19 March 1997, paragraph 40.
215. *Taşkın and Others v. Turkey,* judgment of 10 November 2004, paragraphs 135 and 138.
216. For a short description of the case, see paragraph 15 of the manual.

detrimental consequences on the environment, the Greek authorities had deprived the provisions of Article 6 paragraph 1 of any useful effect.

(c) The right of access to a court guaranteed by Article 6 applies if there is a sufficiently direct link between the environmental problem at issue and the civil right invoked; mere tenuous connections or remote consequences are not sufficient.[217] In case of a serious, specific and imminent environmental risk, Article 6 may be invoked if the danger reaches a degree of probability which makes the outcome of the proceedings directly decisive for the rights of those individuals concerned.[218]

101. Not all national legal systems recognise a specific right to live in a healthy and balanced environment that is directly enforceable by individuals in the courts. In many disputes relating to environmental matters, applicants invoke their more general rights to life, physical integrity or property. In such cases, they have a right of access to a court with all the guarantees under Article 6 of the Convention if the outcome of the dispute is directly decisive for their individual rights. It may be difficult to establish a sufficient link with a "civil right" in cases where the applicants only complain of an environmental risk but have not suffered any damage to their health or property.

102. In the cases of *Balmer-Schafroth and Others v. Switzerland* and *Athanassoglou and Others v. Switzerland*, the Court examined in detail whether the applicants could successfully invoke the right of access to a court in proceedings concerning the granting of operating licences for nuclear power plants. The applicants lived in villages situated in the vicinity of nuclear power stations. In both cases, they objected to the extension of operating licences. They invoked risks to their rights to life, physical integrity and protection of property which they claimed would result from such an extension. According to them, the nuclear power plants did not meet current safety standards and the risk of an accident occurring was greater than usual. In both cases, the Federal Council dismissed all the objections as being unfounded and granted the operating licences. Before the Court, the applicants

---

217. *Balmer-Schafroth and Others v. Switzerland* [GC], paragraph 40.
218. *Balmer-Schafroth and Others v. Switzerland* [GC], paragraph 40; *Taşkın and Others v. Turkey*, paragraph 130.

complained in both cases of a lack of access to a court to challenge the granting of operating licences by the Swiss Federal Council as under Swiss law, they had no possibility of appealing against such decisions. The Court recognised in both cases that there had been a genuine and serious dispute between the applicants and the decision-making authorities on the extension of operating licences for the nuclear power plants. The applicants had a "right" recognised under Swiss law to have their life, physical integrity and property adequately protected from the risks entailed by the use of nuclear energy. The Court found that the decisions at issue were of a judicial character. It had therefore to determine whether the outcome of the proceedings in question had been directly decisive for the rights asserted by the applicants, i.e. whether the link between the public authorities' decisions and the applicants' rights to life, physical integrity and protection of property was sufficiently close to bring Article 6 into play.

103. In the *Balmer-Schafroth and Others v. Switzerland* case the Court found that the applicants had not established a direct link between the operating conditions of the power station and the right to protection of their physical integrity as they had failed to show that the operation of the power station had exposed them personally to a danger that was not only serious but also specific and, above all, imminent. In the absence of such a finding, the effects on the population of the measures which could have been taken regarding security had therefore remained hypothetical. Consequently, neither the dangers nor the remedies had been established with the degree of probability that made the outcome of the proceedings directly decisive within the meaning of the Court's case-law for the right relied on by the applicants. The connection between the Federal Council's decision and the right invoked by the applicants had been too tenuous and remote. The Court ruled therefore that Article 6 was not applicable.

104. The Court reached the same conclusion in the *Athanassoglou and Others v. Switzerland* case.[219] The Court emphasised that the applicants were alleging not so much a specific and imminent danger in their personal regard as a general danger in relation to all nuclear power plants. The Court considered that the outcome of the procedure before the Federal Council was decisive for the general question as to whether the operating licence of the power plant should

---

219. *Athanassoglou and Others v. Greece* [GC], paragraph 54.

be extended, but not for the "determination" of any "civil right", such as the rights to life, physical integrity and protection of property, which Swiss law conferred on the applicants in their individual capacity. The Court thus found Article 6 not to be applicable.

(d) Environmental associations which are entitled to bring proceedings in the national legal system to defend the interests of their members may invoke the right of access to a court when they seek to defend the economic interests of their members (e.g. their personal assets and lifestyle). However, they will not necessarily enjoy a right of access to a court when they are only defending a broad public interest.[220]

105. According to the case-law of the Court, environmental associations may invoke the right of access to a court provided that the proceedings which they bring concern "civil rights" falling within the scope of Article 6 paragraph 1 of the Convention and thus go beyond the general public interest to protect the environment.

106. The Court addressed this issue in the case of *Gorraiz Lizarraga and Others v. Spain*. One of the applicants in this case was an association which had brought proceedings against plans to build a dam in Itoiz, a village of the province of Navarre, which would result in three nature reserves and a number of small villages being flooded. The *Audiencia Nacional* partly allowed their application and ordered the suspension of the work. The parliament of the Autonomous Community of Navarre later passed Law No. 9/1996 on natural sites in Navarre, which amended the rules applicable to conservation areas in nature reserves and effectively allowed work on the dam to continue. Following an appeal on points of law, the Supreme Court reduced the scale of the dam. The State and the Autonomous Government argued that they were unable to execute that judgment in the light of the Autonomous Community's Law No. 9/1996. The *Audiencia Nacional* asked the Constitutional Court to rule on a preliminary question by the applicant association as to the constitutionality of certain provisions of this law. The Constitutional Court found the law in question to be constitutional.

---

220. *Gorraiz Lizarraga and Others v. Spain*, judgment of 27 April 2004, paragraphs 46 and 47.

107. Relying on Article 6 paragraph 1, the applicants submitted that they had not had a fair hearing. They had been prevented from taking part in the proceedings concerning the referral to the Constitutional Court of the preliminary question, whereas the State and State Counsel's Office had been able to submit observations to the Constitutional Court. The government contested the applicability of Article 6 arguing that the dispute did not concern pecuniary or subjective rights of the association, but only a general question of legality and collective rights. The Court rejected this view. Although the dispute was partly about the defence of the general interest, the association also complained about a concrete and direct threat to its personal possessions and the way of life of its members. Since the action was, at least partly, "pecuniary" and "civil" in nature, the association was entitled to rely on Article 6 paragraph 1. The Court stressed that the judicial review by the Constitutional Court had been the only means for the applicants to challenge, albeit indirectly, the interference with their property and way of life. However, the Court found that there had been no violation of Article 6 paragraph 1.

(e) Where public authorities have to determine complex questions of environmental and economic policy, they must ensure that the decision-making process takes account of the rights and interests of the individuals whose rights under Articles 2 and 8 may be affected. Where such individuals consider that their interests have not been given sufficient weight in the decision-making process, they should be able to appeal to a court.[221]

108. The Court has emphasised the importance of the right of access to a court also in the context of Article 8 of the Convention. When complex issues of environmental and economic policy are at stake, the decision-making process leading to measures of interference must be fair and such as to afford due respect to the interests of the individuals concerned. In *Hatton and Others v. the United Kingdom*[222] and in *Taşkın and Others v. Turkey*,[223] the Court recognised that environmental and economic policy must also be able to appeal to the courts against any decision, act or omission where they consider that

---

221. *Taşkın and Others v. Turkey,* judgment of 10 November 2004, paragraph 119.
222. For a short description of the case, see paragraph 28 of the manual.
223. *Taşkın and Others v. Turkey,* paragraph 119. For a short description of the case, see paragraph 26 of the manual.

their interests or their comments have not been given sufficient weight in the decision-making process. Hence, a fair decision-making process in environmental matters, required under Article 8, includes the right to access to court. This principle was confirmed additionally in *Öçkan and Others v. Turkey, Dubetska and Others v. Ukraine, Grimkovskaya v. Urkaine,* and *Tătar v. Romania.*

109. Interestingly, in *Tătar v. Romania* the Court indicated that it should not only be possible to seek redress in court against an improper decision-making process, but also against individual scientific studies requested by the public authorities and to seize a court if necessary documents have not been made available publicly.[224] In this respect the right to access to a court based on Articles 2 and 8 appears broader than that of Article 6. The rights in Articles 2 and 8 do not require that the outcome of the court proceedings need to be decisive for the rights of the applicant or that there must be the possibility of grave danger.[225]

110. In the case of *Giacomelli v. Italy* the Court pointed out again that the decision-making process had to be fair and show due regard for the interests of the individual protected by Article 8. It stressed again that the individuals concerned need to have had the opportunity to appeal to the courts against any decision, act or omission where they considered that their interest or their comments have not been given sufficient weight in the decision-making process.[226] In this case, the Court criticised the entire decision-making process and noted that it was impossible for any citizens concerned to submit their own observations to the judicial authorities and, where appropriate, obtain an order for the suspension of a dangerous activity.[227]

111. The case of *Grimkovskaya v. Urkaine*[228] enlightens the scope of the protection afforded by the procedural rights of Article 8. In this case the absence of the individual's ability to challenge an official act or omission affecting her rights before an independent authority was one of the three factors that led to the Court's finding of a violation of Article 8. The Court held that the applicant's civil claim against the local authorities was prematurely dismissed by the domestic courts.

---

224. *Tătar v. Romania,* paragraphs 113, 116-117 and 119.
225. *Öçkan and Others v. Turkey,* judgment of 28 March 2006 (in French only), paragraphs 39 and 44. *Tătar v. Romania,* 27 January 2009 (in French only), paragraphs 88 and 119.
226. *Giacomelli v. Italy,* paragraph 82.
227. *Giacomelli v. Italy,* paragraph 94.
228. For a short description of the case, see paragraph 22 of the manual.

The reasoning contained in their judgments was too short and it did not include a direct response to the applicant's main arguments, on the basis of which she had sought to establish the local authorities' liability. Hence it was not the lack of access to an independent complaints authority, but the manner in which this authority dealt with the applicant's complaint that led the Court to find a breach of Article 8. Notably, the Court explicitly referred to the standards of the Aarhus Convention to consider whether it provided a meaningful complaints mechanism.[229]

(f) In addition to the right of access to a court as described above, Article 13 guarantees that persons, who have an arguable claim that their rights and freedoms as set forth in the Convention have been violated, must have an effective remedy before a national authority.[230]

(g) The protection afforded by Article 13 does not go so far as to require any particular form of remedy. The State has a margin of appreciation in determining how it gives effect to its obligations under this provision. The nature of the right at stake has implications for the type of remedy which the state is required to provide. Where for instance violations of the rights enshrined in Article 2 are alleged, compensation for economic and non-economic loss should in principle be possible as part of the range of redress available. However, neither Article 13 nor any other provision of the Convention guarantees an individual a right to secure the prosecution and conviction of those responsible.[231]

112. The objective of Article 13 of the Convention is to provide a means whereby individuals can obtain appropriate relief at the national level for violations of their Convention rights so as to avoid having to bring their case before the European Court of Human Rights. States enjoy a certain margin of appreciation as to how they provide remedies within their own legal systems. However, whatever form is chosen, the remedy must be effective.

---

229. *Grimkovskaya v. Ukraine,* paragraphs 69-72.
230. *Leander v. Sweden,* judgment of 26 March 1987, paragraph 77.
231. *Öneryıldız v. Turkey* [GC], paragraph 147.

113. The Court has held that the protection afforded by Article 13 must extend to anyone with an "arguable claim" that his or her rights or freedoms under the Convention have been infringed.[232] It is not necessary for a violation of a right to have been established. The individuals concerned must, however, be able to demonstrate that they have grievances which fall within the scope of one of the Convention rights and which can be regarded as "arguable" in terms of the Convention. The Court has not defined the concept of arguability which is to be interpreted on a case-by-case basis.

114. The Court has developed the following general principles for the application and interpretation of Article 13:[233]

> where an individual has an arguable claim to be the victim of a violation of the rights set forth in the Convention, he or she should have a remedy before a national authority in order both to have the claim decided and, if appropriate, to obtain redress;
>
> the authority referred to in Article 13 does not have to be a judicial authority. However, if it is not, its powers and the guarantees which it affords are relevant in determining whether the remedy before it is effective; this means that it should be composed of members who are impartial and who enjoy safeguards of independence and it should be competent to decide on the merits of the claim and, if appropriate, provide redress;
>
> although no single remedy may itself entirely satisfy the requirements of Article 13, a combination of remedies provided for under domestic law may do so;
>
> Article 13 does not require that remedies should include the possibility of challenging a State's laws before a national authority on the ground that they are contrary to the Convention or equivalent domestic norms.

115. The nature of the right in respect of which a remedy is sought might have implications for the type of remedy which the state is required to provide under Article 13. In the case of alleged violations

---

232. *Klass and Others v. Germany,* judgment of 6 September 1978, paragraph 64; *Silver and Others v. the United Kingdom,* judgment of 25 March 1983, paragraph 113.
233. E.g. *Leander v. Sweden,* paragraph 77.

of the right to life (Article 2), the Court has established high standards for evaluating the effectiveness of domestic remedies. These include the duty to carry out a thorough and effective investigation, a duty that also follows, as a procedural requirement, from Article 2 (see above chapter I under principles e) - g)). Failure to act by government officials whose duty it is to investigate will undermine the effectiveness of any other remedy that may have existed at the material time. There must be a mechanism for establishing the liability of State officials or bodies for acts or omissions. The families of victims must, in principle, receive compensation that reflects the pain, stress, anxiety and frustration suffered in circumstances giving rise to claims under this article.[234]

116. In cases concerning environmental matters, applicants may typically seek remedies under Article 13 for alleged breaches of the right to life (Article 2 of the Convention), the right to respect for private and family life (Article 8 of the Convention) or the right to the protection of property (Article 1 of Protocol No. 1 to the Convention) (see chapters I, II and III of the manual).

117. In *Hatton and Others v. the United Kingdom*[235] the Court considered whether the applicants had had a remedy at national level to enforce their Convention rights under Article 8. As stated before, the applicants complained of excessive night-time noise from airplanes landing and taking off from Heathrow Airport. They argued that the scope of judicial review provided by English courts had been too limited. At the time, the courts were only competent to examine whether the authorities had acted irrationally, unlawfully or manifestly unreasonably (classic English public-law concepts). The English courts had not been able to consider whether the claimed increase in night flights represented a justifiable limitation on the right to respect for private and family lives or for the homes of those who lived near Heathrow Airport. The Court accordingly held that there had been a violation of Article 13.

118. In *Öneryıldız v. Turkey*[236] the Court examined the adequacy of criminal and administrative investigations that had been carried out following a methane-gas explosion on a waste-collection site. The national authorities carried out criminal and administrative

---

234. *Keenan v. the United Kingdom*, judgment of 3 April 2001, paragraphs 123-130.
235. For a short description of the case, see paragraph 28 of the manual.
236. For a short description of the case, see paragraph 4 of the manual.

investigations, following which the mayors of Ümraniye and Istanbul were brought before the courts, the former for failing to comply with his duty to have the illegal dwellings surrounding the said tip destroyed and the latter for failing to make the rubbish tip safe or order its closure. They were both convicted of "negligence in the exercise of their duties" and sentenced to very low fines and the minimum three-month prison sentence, which was later commuted to a fine. The applicant complained of important shortcomings in the criminal and administrative investigations. After finding a violation of Article 2, the Court examined the complaints also under Article 13. It noted that remedies for alleged violations of the right to life should allow for compensation of any pecuniary and non-pecuniary damages suffered by the individuals concerned. However, neither Article 13 nor any other provision of the Convention guarantees an applicant the right to secure the prosecution and conviction of a third party or the right to "private revenge". The Court found violations of Article 13 both with regard to the right to life (Article 2) and the protection of property (Article 1 of Protocol No. 1).

119. As regards the complaint under Article 2, the Court considered that the administrative law remedy available appeared sufficient to enforce the substance of the applicant's complaints regarding the death of his relatives and was capable of affording him adequate redress. However, the Court underlined that the timely payment of a final award should be considered an essential element of a remedy under Article 13. It noted that the Administrative Court had taken four years, eleven months and ten days to reach its decision and even then the damages awarded (which were only for non-pecuniary loss) were never actually paid to the applicant. The Court concluded that the administrative proceedings had not provided the applicant with an effective remedy in respect of the State's failure to protect the lives of his relatives.

120. As regards the complaint under Article 1 of Protocol No. 1, the decision on compensation had been unduly delayed and the amount awarded in respect of the destruction of household goods never paid. The Court therefore ruled that the applicant had been denied an effective remedy also in respect of the alleged breach of Article 1 of Protocol No. 1.

121. In the case of *Budayeva and Others v. Russia*, the applicants complained of the lack of any effective remedy through which to make their claims, as required by Article 13 of the Convention. The Court found that the principles developed in relation to the judicial response to accidents resulting from dangerous activities also applied in the area of disaster relief.[237] It pointed out in particular that "in relation to fatal accidents arising out of dangerous activities which fall within the responsibility of the State, Article 2 requires the authorities to carry out of their own motion an investigation, satisfying certain minimum conditions, into the cause of the loss of life. Without such an investigation, the individual concerned may not be in a position to use any remedy available to him for obtaining relief. This is because the knowledge necessary to elucidate facts, such as those in issue in the instant case, is often in the sole hands of state officials or authorities. Accordingly, the Court's task under Article 13 is to determine whether the applicant's exercise of an effective remedy was frustrated on account of the manner in which the authorities discharged their procedural obligation under Article 2" (see *Öneryıldız v. Turkey*, paragraphs 90, 93-94 and 149). The Court considered that "these principles must equally apply in the context of the State's alleged failure to exercise their responsibilities in the area of disaster relief".[238] In this case, the Court observed that the state's failings had given rise to a violation of Article 2 because of the lack of an adequate judicial response, as required in the event of alleged infringements of the right to life. When assessing the procedural aspect of the right to life, the Court addressed not only the lack of a criminal investigation but also the absence of other means for the applicants to secure redress for the alleged failure. Accordingly, it did not consider it necessary to examine the complaint separately under Article 13.

(h) Environmental protection concerns may in addition to Articles 6 and 13 impact the interpretation of other procedural articles, such as Article 5 which sets out the rules for detention and arrest of person. The Court has found that in the case of offences against the environment, like the massive spilling of oil by ships, a strong legal interest of the public exists to prosecute those responsible. The Court recognised

---

237. *Budayeva and Others v. Russia*, paragraph 142.
238. *Budayeva and Others v. Russia*, paragraphs 192 and 193.

that maritime environmental protection law has evolved constantly. Hence, it is in the light of those "new realities" that the Convention articles need to be interpreted. Consequently, environmental damage can be of a degree that justifies arrest and detention, as well as the imposition of a substantial amount of bail.

122. The case of *Mangouras v. Spain*[239] is a telling example of the Court's reflex on an increased international concern for environmental protection. It is concerned with the correct interpretation of Article 5 paragraph 3 of the Convention. The applicant was the captain of the ship Prestige, which had been sailing off the Spanish coast in November 2002 when its hull had sprung a leak, spilling its cargo of fuel oil into the Atlantic Ocean and causing an ecological disaster whose effects on marine flora and fauna had lasted for several months and spread as far as the French coast. The case related to the applicant's complaints concerning his pre-trial detention for offences including an offence against natural resources and the environment and the bail (3 million euro) set to ensure that he would attend his trial. On the matter of whether the sum set for bail was proportionate to the applicant's personal circumstances and the seriousness of the offence (offences against the environment and, in particular, the marine environment), the Chamber considered that:

the amount of bail in the instant case, although high, was not disproportionate in view of the legal interest being protected, the seriousness of the offence and the disastrous consequences, both environmental and economic, stemming from the spillage of the ship's cargo.[240]

The Court considered that there is growing and legitimate concern both in Europe and internationally about offences against the environment. It noted in this regard the states' powers and obligations to prevent marine pollution and bring those responsible to justice.[241] The Court made explicit reference to the law of the sea which justified the raised perseverance of the domestic courts to bring those responsible to justice.

---

239. *Mangouras v. Spain*, judgment of 8 January 2009.
240. *Mangouras v. Spain*, paragraph 44.
241. *Mangouras v. Spain*, paragraph 41.

123. The Grand Chamber[242] agreed with the Chamber on all points. It stressed that the amount of bail can take into account the seriousness of the damage caused and the professional environment of the accused, i.e. the ability of insurances and his employer to provide for the bail. The Grand Chamber also took note of the tendency to use criminal law as means of enforcing the environmental obligations imposed by European and international law. Moreover, the Court considered that "these new realities have to be taken into account in interpreting the requirements of Article 5 paragraph 3". The Grand Chamber agreed that if there are very significant implications in terms of both criminal and civil liability, like in the present case for instance "marine pollution on a seldom-seen scale causing huge environmental damage," the authorities can adjust the bail accordingly. In support of this position the Court took into account the practice of the International Tribunal for the Law of the Sea in fixing its deposits.[243] The Court found that there had been no violation of Article 5 paragraph 3 of the Convention.

124. The case is remarkable as the Court, taking into account developing international environmental regulations, revised its existing case-law, i.e. it found that a bail should not always be determined on the individual capacity of the accused to provide for it. The case, once again, underlines the direct impact of the development of international environmental standards and legal norms on the protection of human rights as afforded by the Court.

---

242. *Mangouras v. Spain* [GC], judgment of 28 September 2010, paragraph 81.
243. *Mangouras v. Spain* [GC], paragraphs 86-88.

Chapter VII: Principles from the Court's case-law: territorial scope of the Convention's application

ARTICLE 1
OBLIGATION TO RESPECT HUMAN RIGHTS

The High Contracting Parties shall secure to everyone within their jurisdiction the rights and freedoms defined in Section I of this Convention.

(a) In general, the Convention applies to a state's own territory. The notion of "jurisdiction" for the purpose of Article 1 of the Convention must be considered to reflect the term's meaning in public international law.[244] Hence, the jurisdictional competence under Article 1 is territorial. Jurisdiction is presumed to be exercised normally throughout the States' territory.[245]

> 125. However, the presumption of the exercise of jurisdiction within one's territory is not irrevocable. When a Contracting Party is not capable of exercising authority on the whole of its territory by a constraining *de facto* situation, such a situation reduces the scope of jurisdiction in that the undertaking given by the State under Article 1 must be considered by the Court only in the light of the Contracting State's positive obligations towards persons within its territory.[246]

(b) The concept of "jurisdiction" in Article 1 of the Convention is not necessarily restricted to the national territory of the High Contracting Parties. In exceptional circumstances, the acts of Contracting Parties performed or producing effects outside their territories can constitute an exercise of jurisdiction within the meaning of Article 1.[247]

---

244. *Gentilhomme, Schaff-Benhadji and Zerouki v. France*, judgment of 14 May 2002 (French only) paragraph 20; *Banković and Others v. Belgium and 16 Other Contracting States* [GC], decision of admissibility of 12.12.2001, paragraphs 59-61; *Assanidzé v. Georgia* [GC], judgment of 8 April 2004, paragraph 137.

245. *Al-Skeini and Others v. the United Kingdom* [GC], judgment of 7 July 2011; *Banković and Others v. Belgium and 16 Other Contracting States* [GC], decision of 12 December 2001, paragraph 61.

246. *Ilaşcu and Others v. Moldova and Russia* [GC], paragraphs 313, 333.

247. The Court found that to be the case, for instance, when a Contracting Party exercises effective overall control over a foreign territory, or authority and control over an individual outside its own territory. See, *inter alia*, *Al-Skeini and Others v. the United Kingdom* [GC], paragraphs 131 and following; *Issa and Others v. Turkey*, judgment of 16 November 2004, paragraphs 68 and 71; *Isaak v. Turkey*, decision of admissibility of 28 September 2006; *Ilaşcu and Others v. Moldova and Russia* [GC], paragraphs 314 and 318. It may also be noted that, although this is not a form of extraterritorial jurisdiction, that in a number of cases concerning extradition or expulsion, the Court found that a Contracting Party may be responsible for acts or omissions on its own territory which have an effect in breach of the Convention outside its territory, if such consequences are foreseeable.

126. A key case with regard to the notion of the jurisdiction is *Loizidou v. Turkey*, in which the Court stated that:

"jurisdiction" under Article 1 of the Convention is not restricted to the national territory of the Contracting States. Accordingly, the responsibility of Contracting States can be involved by acts and omissions of their authorities which produce effects outside their own territory.[248]

127. In *Al-Skeini and Others v. the United Kingdom*, the Court, engaging in a comprehensive review of its past case-law, identified a number of exceptional circumstances capable of giving rise to the exercise of jurisdiction outside a State's own territorial boundaries. It stressed, however, that:

in each case, the question whether exceptional circumstances exist which require and justify a finding by the Court that the State was exercising jurisdiction extra-territorially must be determined with reference to the particular facts.[249]

(c) The Court has not decided on cases relating to environmental protection which raise extra-territorial and transboundary issues. The Court has produced, in different contexts, ample case-law elaborating the principles of the extra-territorial and transboundary application of the Convention, which could be potentially relevant for environmental issues. However, as they have been developed under very different factual circumstances, it will be up to the Court to determine if and how they can be applied to cases concerning the environment.

128. The Court came close to considering the extraterritorial application in environmental cases with the nuclear test cases against the United Kingdom, e.g. *L.C.B v. the United Kingdom*[250] and *McGinley and Egan v. the United Kingdom.*[251] In those cases the Court

---

248. *Loizidou v. Turkey (merits)* [GC], judgment of 18 December 1996, paragraph 52. The position was reiterated in a number of other cases: e.g. *Cyprus v. Turkey (merits)* [GC], judgment of 10 May 2001, paragraphs 76, 77, 81. *Al-Skeini and Others v. the United Kingdom* [GC], paragraph 131, *Issa and Others v. Turkey*, judgment of 16 November 2004, paragraph 68, *Ilaşcu and Others v. Moldova and Russia* [GC], paragraph 314.

249. *Al-Skeini and Others v. the United Kingdom* [GC], paragraph 132.

250. *L.C.B v. the United Kingdom*, judgment of 9 June 1998.

251. *McGinley and Egan v. the United Kingdom*, judgment of 9 June 1998.

had to consider the health impact of British nuclear testing upon service members and their children on the Christmas Islands in the Pacific and which were conducted partially after the transfer of sovereignty over those islands to Australia in 1957. In both cases, the application of the Convention outside the territory was not discussed. The applications were considered inadmissible for other reasons.

(d)In addition, it may be recalled that the Court in its case-law has made reference to international environmental law standards and principles, which by their very nature may have transboundary characteristics.[252]

---

252. For examples see Appendix III of this manual.

SECTION B – PRINCIPLES DERIVED FROM THE EUROPEAN SOCIAL CHARTER AND THE REVISED EUROPEAN SOCIAL CHARTER

The European Social Charter (referred to below as "the Charter") was adopted in 1961. It sets out social and economic rights and freedoms and establishes a supervisory mechanism guaranteeing their respect by the States Parties. Following its revision in 1996, the revised European Social Charter came into force in 1999 and it is gradually replacing the initial treaty. At present, the two treaties coexist and are interlinked. Forty-three member States[253] have either ratified the Social Charter or its revised version. Upon ratification States Parties indicate in accordance with Article A of the Charter which provisions they intend to accept.

The European Committee of Social Rights (referred to below as "the Committee") rules on the conformity of national law and practice with the Charter. Its fifteen independent members are elected by the Council of Europe Committee of Ministers for a period of six years, renewable once. The Committee delivers its rulings in the framework of two procedures: a reporting procedure and a collective complaints procedure.

On the basis of yearly reports submitted by the States Parties concerning a selection of the accepted provisions and indicating how they implement the Charter in law and in practice, the Committee determines whether or not the national situations are in conformity with the Charter.[254]

Under an Additional Protocol to the Charter, which came into force in 1998, national trade unions and employers' organisations as well as certain European trade unions and employers' organisations and certain international NGOs are entitled to lodge complaints of violations of the Charter with the

---

253. States Parties of the 1961 Charter: Austria, Belgium, Croatia, Cyprus, Czech Republic, Denmark, Finland, France, Germany, Greece, Hungary, Iceland, Ireland, Italy, Latvia, Luxembourg, Malta, Netherlands, Norway, Poland, Portugal, Slovak Republic, Spain, Sweden, "the former Yugoslav Republic of Macedonia", Turkey and the United Kingdom.
States Parties of the 1996 Revised Charter: Albania, Andorra, Armenia, Austria, Azerbaijan, Belgium, Bosnia and Herzegovina, Bulgaria, Cyprus, Estonia, Finland, France, Georgia, Hungary, Ireland, Italy, Lithuania, Malta, Moldova, Montenegro, Netherlands, Norway, Portugal, Romania, Russian Federation, Serbia, Slovak Republic, Slovenia, Sweden, Turkey and Ukraine.
The following States have neither ratified the 1961 Charter nor the 1996 Revised Charter: Liechtenstein, Monaco, San Marino and Switzerland. However Liechtenstein and Switzerland have signed the 1961 Charter and Monaco and San Marino have signed the 1996 Revised Charter.
254. Article 24 of the Charter as amended by the 1991 Turin Protocol.

Committee. In addition, national NGOs may lodge complaints if the State concerned makes a declaration to this effect.

At present, 66 collective complaints[255] have been examined by the European Committee of Social Rights. Once the Committee has reached a decision on a collective complaint, it then systematically examines the issues raised by the complaint in all the States Parties to the Charter when it next considers the reports on the relevant provision.[256]

The Committee, which is a quasi-judicial body,[257] has over the years developed a "case-law"[258] which consists of all the sources in which the Committee sets out its interpretation of the Charter provisions.[259] These include conclusions arising from the reporting procedure, statements of interpretation contained in the volumes of conclusions and the decisions on collective complaints.

The Charter has inspired the formulation of many of the provisions of the EU Charter of Fundamental Rights. Having entered into force with the Treaty of Lisbon on 1 December 2009, at present no cases concerning the EU Charter provisions have yet been brought before the European Court of Justice which is responsible for their interpretation.

More information regarding the Charter and the Committee and notably the full text of the 1961 Charter and the 1996 Revised Charter as well as the practical conditions to lodge a collective complaint with the Committee are to be found on the following website: www.coe.int/SocialCharter.

---

255. As of August 2011.
256. Régis Brillat, *The Supervisory Machinery of the European Social Charter: Recent Developments and their Impact*, in Social Rights in Europe, pp. 36-37 (Gráinne de Búrca & Bruno de Witte eds., Oxford Univ. Press, 2005).
257. Régis Brillat, *The Supervisory Machinery of the European Social Charter: Recent Developments and their Impact*, in Social Rights in Europe pp. 32-37 (Gráinne de Búrca & Bruno de Witte eds., Oxford Univ. Press, 2005).
258. "Case-law" is the term used by the Committee itself, see Régis Brillat, *The Supervisory Machinery of the European Social Charter: Recent Developments and their Impact*, in Social Rights in Europe pp. 32-37 (Gráinne de Búrca & Bruno de Witte eds., Oxford Univ. Press, 2005).
259. Since 2008 the interpretation by the Committee of the different provisions of the revised Charter is presented in a "Digest of the case-law" (September 2008) prepared by the Secretariat. www.coe.int/t/dghl/monitoring/socialcharter/Digest/DigestSept2008_en.pdf. The content is however not binding on the Committee but is intended to give an indication to national authorities of how they are expected to implement the Charter provisions.

There is also a database providing the full text of all the conclusions, statements of interpretation and decisions of the Committee at: http://hudoc.esc.coe.int/esc2008/query.asp?language=en.

Chapter I: Right to protection of health and the environment

ARTICLE 11
RIGHT TO THE PROTECTION OF HEALTH

Part I

Everyone has the right to benefit from any measures enabling him to enjoy the highest possible standard of health attainable.

Part II

With a view to ensuring the effective exercise of the right to protection of health, the Parties undertake, either directly or in co-operation with public or private organisations, to take appropriate measures designed *inter alia*:

- to remove as far as possible the causes of ill-health;
- to provide advisory and educational facilities for the promotion of health and the encouragement of individual responsibility in matters of health;
- to prevent as far as possible epidemic, endemic and other diseases.

(a) Article 11 on the right to protection of health has been interpreted by the Committee as including the right to a healthy environment.[260] The Committee has noted the complementarity between the right to health under Article 11 of the Charter and Articles 2 and 3 of the European Convention on Human Rights.[261] As a consequence, several Committee conclusions on State reports regarding the right to health, specifically indicate that the measures required under Article 11, paragraph 1 should be designed to remove the causes of ill health resulting from environmental threats such as pollution.[262]

129. The inclusion of environmental protection under Article 11 was outlined by the Committee in its decision on complaint *Marangopoulos Foundation for Human Rights (MFHR) v. Greece.*[263] The Committee took the opportunity of this complaint to reaffirm that the Charter is a living instrument, whose purpose is to protect rights not merely theoretically but also in fact.[264] The rights and freedoms set out in the Charter should therefore be interpreted in the light of current conditions.[265] By taking into account the growing link made by States Party to the Social Charter and other international bodies between the protection of health and a healthy environment, the Committee identified environmental protection as one of the key elements of the right to health under Article 11 of the Charter.[266]

(b) States are responsible for activities which are harmful to the environment whether they are carried out by the public authorities themselves or by a private company.

---

260. *Marangopoulos Foundation for Human Rights (MFHR) v. Greece*, Decision of 6 December 2006 (Merits), paragraphs 195-196.
261. 2005 Conclusions XVII-2, Volume 1, General Introduction, paragraph 5; *Marangopoulos v. Greece*, paragraph 202.
262. Mirja Trilsch, *European Committee of Social Rights: The right to a healthy environment*, International Journal of Constitutional Law, Vol. 7 p. 535 (July 2009).
263. *Marangopoulos v. Greece* is the first and at present the only collective complaint decision concerning the right to a healthy environment.
264. The Committee adopted this dynamic interpretative approach in its very first collective complaint decision from 1999, *International Commission of Jurists v. Portugal*, Decision of 6 December 2006 (Merits), paragraph 32. This decision echoes the approach and the language used by the European Court of Human Rights in its judgment *Tyrer v. The United Kingdom*, judgment of 25 April 1978, paragraph 31.
265. *Marangopoulos v. Greece*, paragraph 194.
266. *Marangopoulos v. Greece*, paragraph 195.

130. In the Marangopoulos case, the Greek Government claimed that the mining operations were undertaken by a private entity for whose actions the State could not be held accountable. The Committee, however, pointed out that, regardless of the company's legal status, Greece was required to ensure compliance with its undertakings under the Charter.[267]

131. The Committee's jurisdiction *ratione temporis* had to be considered since the complaint concerned air pollution which partly preceded 1 August 1998 when the Protocol establishing the collective complaint procedure had not yet entered into force as regards Greece. However, the Committee decided to hold Greece accountable in light of international norms on State responsibility, notably Article 14 of the 2001 Articles on the Responsibility of States for Internationally Wrongful Acts produced by the International Law Commission,[268] which provides that when a State is under an international obligation to take preventive action against a certain event, and this event occurs, the State remains in breach over the entire period during which the event continues. The Committee found that there might be a breach of the obligation to prevent damage arising from air pollution for as long as the pollution continues, and that the breach might even be compounded, progressively, if sufficient measures were not taken to put an end to it.[269]

(c) Overcoming pollution is an objective that can only be achieved gradually. Nevertheless, States must strive to attain this objective within a reasonable time, by showing measurable progress and making best possible use of the resources at their disposal.[270] The measures taken by States with a view to overcoming pollution are assessed with reference to their national legislation and undertakings entered into with regard to the European Union and the United Nations[271] and in terms of how the relevant law is applied in practice.

---

267. *Marangopoulos v. Greece*, paragraph 192.
268. See "Glossary". Appendix I.
269. *Marangopoulos v. Greece*, paragraph 193.
270. *Marangopoulos v. Greece*, paragraph 204.
271. Conclusions XV-2, Italy, Article 11 paragraph 3, "Reduction of environmental risks".

132. While acknowledging in the Marangopoulos case that the use of lignite and, by extension, its mining serve legitimate objectives under the Charter (such as energy independence, access to electricity at a reasonable cost, and economic growth), the Committee, nonetheless, identified several areas in which the State's efforts fell short of Greece's national and international undertakings to overcome pollution, which, in turn, had resulted in a failure to protect the health of the population. The Committee assessed Greece's overall efforts to overcome pollution in the light of its international undertakings for emission control and found that the National Allocation Plan for greenhouse gas emissions drawn up by Greece in accordance with EU law[272] was much less demanding than the binding targets for Greece under the Kyoto Protocol.[273] Based on these and other facts before it, the Committee, therefore, found no real evidence of Greece's commitment to improving the situation as regards to air pollution within a reasonable time.[274] In this decision, the Committee set a precedent for examining a State party's compliance with its international environmental obligations. The same line of reasoning can now be found in the Committee's conclusions on State reports with regard to the protection of health.[275]

(d) In order to combat air pollution States are required to implement an appropriate strategy which should include the following measures:[276]

– **develop and regularly update sufficiently comprehensive environmental legislation and regulations;[277]**

---

272. Directive 2003/87/EC of the European Parliament and of the Council of 13 October 2003 establishing a scheme for greenhouse gas emission allowance trading within the Community.

273. *Marangopoulos v. Greece,* paragraphs 204 and 206.

274. *Marangopoulos v. Greece,* paragraphs 203 and 205.

275. Conclusion XV-1, Article 11 paragraph 1, for all States. See also Régis Brillat, *The Supervisory Machinery of the European Social Charter: Recent Developments and their Impact,* in Social Rights in Europe, p. 39 (Gráinne de Búrca & Bruno de Witte eds., Oxford Univ. Press, 2005). Among the member states who have also obligations under the Kyoto Protocol Italy has been recently analysed (Conclusions of the 15th cycle: XV 2, Italy, Article 11, paragraph 3)

276. *Marangopoulos v. Greece,* paragraph 203.

277. Conclusions XV-2, Addendum, Slovakia, Article 11, "Reduction of environmental risks".

- take specific steps, such as modifying equipment, introducing threshold values for emissions and measuring air quality, to prevent air pollution at local level[278] and to help to reduce it on a global scale;[279]

- ensure that environmental standards and rules are properly applied, through appropriate supervisory machinery;[280]

- inform and educate the public, including pupils and students at school, about both general and local environmental problems.[281]

> 133. In Marangopoulos, the Committee found that, although the Greek Constitution made protection of the environment an obligation of the State and, at the same time, an individual right, national environmental protection legislation and regulations were well developed and regularly updated, provision was made for the public to be informed and to participate in the decision-making process as required by the Aarhus Convention and limit values had been set for exposure to pollutants arising from lignite mining, the relevant measures were not applied and enforced in an effective manner and the environmental inspectorates were not sufficiently equipped.[282] Noting also shortcomings in the area of health education courses and the organisation of monitoring of health risks,[283] the Committee concluded that, notwithstanding the margin of discretion granted to national authorities in such matters, Greece had not managed "to strike a reasonable balance between the interests of persons living in the lignite mining areas and the general interest," and thus that there had been a violation of Greece's obligations with respect to the right to protection of health under the Charter.[284]

---

278. Conclusions 2005, Volume 2, Moldova, Article 11 paragraph 3, "Reduction of environmental risks".

279. Conclusions XI-2, Italy, Article 11 paragraph 3, "Reduction of environmental risks".

280. *Marangopoulos v. Greece,* paragraphs 203, 209, 210 and 215.

281. Conclusions 2005, Volume 2, Moldova, Article 11 paragraph 2, "health education in schools".

282. *Marangopoulos v. Greece,* paragraphs 205 and 208-216.

283. *Marangopoulos v. Greece,* paragraphs 216 and 219.

284. *Marangopoulos v. Greece,* paragraph 221.

(e) In a State where a part of its energy source derives from nuclear power plants, this State is under the obligation to prevent related hazards for the communities living in the areas of risk. Moreover, all States are required to protect their population against the consequences of nuclear accidents taking place abroad and having an effect within their territory.[285]

134. The Committee has held that the dose limits of radiation on the population should be established in accordance with the 1990 Recommendation of the International Commission for Radiation Protection. For EU member States there is a need to transpose into domestic law "Community Directive 96/29/Euratom on the protection of the health of workers and the general public against the dangers arising from ionising radiation". The assessment of conformity with Article 11 paragraph 3 will vary from one country to another depending on the extent to which energy production is based on nuclear power.[286]

(f) Under Article 11 States must apply a policy which bans the use, production and sale of asbestos and products containing it.[287]

135. The Committee has held that States under Article 11 paragraph 3 must also adopt legislation requiring the owners of residential property and public buildings to search for any asbestos and where appropriate remove it, and imposing obligations on enterprises concerning waste disposals.[288]

---

285. Conclusion XV-2, Volume 1, Denmark, Article 11 paragraph 3, "Reduction of environmental risks".
286. Conclusions XV-2, Volume 1, France, Article 11 paragraph 3, "Reduction of environmental risks".
287. Conclusions XVII-2, Volume 2, Portugal, Article 11 paragraph 3, "Reduction of environmental risks".
288. Conclusions XVII-2, Volume 2, Latvia, Article 11 paragraph 3, "Reduction of environmental risks".

Appendices to the manual

Appendix I: Glossary

Actio popularis   The Latin term *actio popularis* refers to actions taken to obtain remedy by a person or a group in the name of the general public. Those persons or groups are neither themselves victims of a violation nor have been authorised to represent any victims.

Applicant   Any person, non-governmental organisation or group of persons that brings a case before the European Court of Human Rights. The right to raise a complaint with the Court is guaranteed by Article 34 of the European Convention on Human Rights. It is subject to the conditions set out in Article 35 of the Convention.

Aarhus Convention   The Convention on Access to Information, Public Participation in Decision-Making and Access to Justice in Environmental Matters of 1998 (commonly referred to as the Aarhus Convention). The Convention is considered one of the cornerstones of environmental procedural rights in Europe. However, it does not contain substantial environmental rights, but assumes their existence. As of October 2011, there are 45 Parties to the Convention (37 Council of Europe member states), 27 Parties to the Protocol on Pollutant Release (26 Council of Europe member states) and Transfer Registers and 26 Parties to the amendment on public participation in decisions on the deliberate release into the environment and placing on the market of genetically modified organisms (26 Council of Europe member states).

Civil rights   The Court has not sought to provide a comprehensive definition of what is meant by a "civil right or obligation" for the purposes of the Convention. However, it recognised that with regard to environmental pollution, applicants may invoke their rights to have their physical integrity and the enjoyment of their property adequately protected since they are recognised in the national law of most European countries. In addition, an enforceable right to live in a healthy and balanced environment if enshrined in national law can serve to invoke Article 6 Paragraph 1.

Common but differentiated responsibilities principle

This principle is built upon the understanding that states, because they are in different stages of development, have contributed and are contributing to different degrees to environmental pollution and have also distinct technological and financial capabilities. At the same time it recognises that only comprehensive and co-ordinated actions can address the global environmental degradation appropriately. This principle was first stressed in the Rio Declaration (Principle 7) in 1992.

Complainant

Under the European Social Charter a collective complaints mechanism exists (Part IV Article D). Three types of institutions are qualified to submit complaints: international organisations of employers and trade unions, other international non-governmental organisations which have consultative status with the Council of Europe and have been put on a special list; representative national organisations of employers and trade unions within the jurisdiction of the Contracting Party against which they intent to lodge a complaint.

Continuing violation

A continuing violation of the Convention[289] or of the Charter[290] exists whenever a conduct for which the State is responsible is persistent and by virtue of the ongoing conduct the state is breaching its obligations. This also includes sustained inaction of the state where it has a positive obligation to act. However, instantaneous acts that might carry ensuing effects do not in themselves give rise to any possible continuous situation in breach of a provision of the Convention or Charter.

Co-operation/ provision of information principles

These two principles stem from general public international law. In essence, they require states to inform and consult other states that might be affected by various projects, e.g. the construction of a dam or factory. It has been enshrined in numerous bi- and multilateral treaties. It has been reaffirmed, for example, in the ICJ cases of Pulp Mills and Gabcikovo Nagymaros.[291]

---

289. *Loizidou v. Turkey,* judgment of 18 December 1996, Application No. 15318/89, paragraph 41, see also *Veeber v. Estonia,* judgment of 7 November 2002, Application No. 37571/97 and *Dudgeon v. Ireland,* judgment of 22 October 1981, Application No. 7525/76, paragraph 40.

290. *Marangopoulos Foundation for Human Rights (MFHR) v. Greece,* decision on admissibility of 10 October 2005, Complaint No. 30/2005, paragraphs 15-17.

291. Case concerning Pulp Mills on the River Uruguay (*Argentina v. Uruguay*), Judgment of 20 April 2010, ICJ General List 135, available at: www.icj-cij.org/docket/files/135/15877.pdf, *Gabcikovo-Nagymaros Project* (*Hungary v. Slovakia*), Judgment of 25 September 1997, ICJ Reports (1997) 7.

Dangerous activities	The Court uses this notion in the context of Articles 2 and 8 of the Convention, as well as Article 1 of Protocol No. 1 to the Convention. So far, the Court has not given a general definition of the concept. In the context of Article 2 of the Convention, the Court has qualified toxic emissions from a fertiliser factory, waste collection sites or nuclear tests as "dangerous activities", whether carried out by public authorities or private companies, but the concept could encompass a wider range of industrial activities.
	At the international and European level, several instruments refer to the related concept of "hazardous activities. However, although aiming at the protection of human health and the environment, these instruments primarily focus on the technical and procedural aspects of the control of "dangerous" or "hazardous activities" and do not address the question of adverse effects on the effective enjoyment of human rights. Consequently "hazardous" or "dangerous activities" are generally described in relation to the handling of dangerous substances as such.[292] The substances deemed "hazardous" or "dangerous" are usually listed in appendices to those instruments. These substance-related criteria may be coupled with a quantity criterion.[293] If not appearing in the lists, a substance may also be qualified "hazardous" on the basis of indicative criteria, namely the nature of its characteristics. Another way of identifying hazardous substances is to cumulatively apply the substance and the characteristics criteria.[294]
Effective remedy	Article 13 of the Convention states that "everyone whose rights and freedoms as set forth in this Convention are violated shall have an effective remedy before a national authority notwithstanding that the violation has been committed by persons acting in an official capacity". Article 13 seeks to ensure that states fulfil their obligations under the Convention without the need for citizens to take their case to the European Court of Human Rights. It essentially means that anyone who believes that his or her human

---

292. Convention on Civil Liability for Damage resulting from Activities Dangerous to the Environment of 21 June 1993 (ETS No. 150); Bamako Convention on the Ban of the Import into Africa and the Control of Transboundary Movement and Management of Hazardous Wastes within Africa of 30 January 1994; Basel Convention on the Control of Transboundary Movements of Hazardous Wastes and their Disposal of 22 March 1989.
293. Convention on the Transboundary effects of industrial accidents, Helsinki 1992; Council Directive 96/82/EC of 9 December 1996 on the control of major-accident hazards involving dangerous substances – Seveso II.
294. Basel Convention article 1 a) and annex III referring to a list of hazardous characteristics corresponding to the hazard classification system included in the United Nations Recommendations on the Transport of Dangerous Goods (ST/SG/AC.10/1Rev.5, United Nations, New York, 1988).

rights as guaranteed by the Convention have been violated must be able to bring the matter to the attention of the authorities and, if a violation has occurred, to have the situation corrected.

Environment

There is no standard definition of the environment in international law. In addition, neither the Convention nor the Charter nor the "case-law" of the Court and the Committee attempt to define it. The Court's and the Committee's purpose is the protection of human rights enshrined in their respective instruments and to examine individual cases in order to assess whether there has been a violation of one of these rights in specific circumstances. Because of the nature of this task, the Court and the Committee have not had to give a general definition of the environment. In the framework of the Council of Europe, the Convention on Civil Liability for Damage Resulting from Activities Dangerous to the Environment endeavours to define the scope of the concept of the environment. It holds that the environment includes natural resources both abiotic and biotic, such as air, water, soil, fauna and flora and the interaction between the same factors, property which forms part of the cultural heritage; and the characteristic aspects of the landscape. Moreover, the International Court of Justice has attempted to define the notion in its Advisory Opinion on the Legality of the Threat or Use of Nuclear Weapons. It held that "the environment is not an abstraction but represents the living space, the quality of life and the very health of human beings, including generations unborn".[295] Considering the various definitions, it appears to be commonly accepted that the environment includes a wide range of elements including air, water, land, flora and fauna as well as human health and safety and that it is to be protected as part of the more global goal of ensuring sustainable development (see also Rio Declaration).

Equitable utilisation/ equitability principle

The principles of "equitable utilisation" and "equitability" are closely related. They hold that states need to co-operate with a view to controlling, preventing, reducing or eliminating adverse environmental effects which may result from the utilisation of shared natural resources. Moreover, the benefits from the use of those resources must be shared equitably. The Lac Lanoux arbitral award confirmed this principle.

---

295. *Legality of the Threat or Use of Nuclear Weapons*, Advisory opinion of 8 July 1996, ICJ Reports (1996) 226, paragraph 29.

European Committee of Social Rights ("the Committee")	The European Committee of Social Rights ascertains whether countries have honoured the undertakings set out in the Charter. Its fifteen independent, impartial members are elected by the Council of Europe Committee of Ministers for a term of six years, renewable once. Every year the States Parties submit a report indicating how they implement the Charter in law and in practice. The Committee examines the reports and decides whether or not the situations in the countries concerned are in conformity with the Charter. Its decisions, known as "conclusions", are published every year. In addition, it hears individual complaints (see *Complainant*). If a state takes no action on a Committee decision to the effect that it does not comply with the Charter, the Committee of Ministers addresses a recommendation to that state, asking it to remedy the situation in law and/or in practice.
European Convention on Human Rights ("the Convention")	The full title is the "Convention for the Protection of Human Rights and Fundamental Freedoms", usually referred to as "the Convention". It was adopted in 1950 and entered into force in 1953. The full text of the Convention and its additional Protocols is available in 29 languages at www.echr.coe.int. The chart of signatures and ratifications as well as the text of declarations and reservations made by states parties can be consulted at http://conventions.coe.int. Currently, it has 47 members.
European Court of Human Rights ("the Court")	The European Court of Human Rights was set up in Strasbourg by the Council of Europe member states in 1959 to deal with alleged violations of the 1950 European Convention on Human Rights. Since 1 November 1998 it has sat as a full-time Court composed of an equal number of judges to that of the High Contracting Parties to the Convention. The Court examines the admissibility and merits of applications submitted to it. It sits in a single-judge formation, in committees of three judges, in Chambers of seven judges and in exceptional cases as Grand Chamber of seventeen judges. The Committee of Ministers of the Council of Europe supervises the execution of the Court's judgments.
European Social Charter ("the Charter")	The Charter is a Council of Europe treaty which guarantees social and economic human rights pertaining to housing, health, education, employment, legal and social protection, free movement of persons, and non-discrimination. It was adopted in 1961 and revised in 1996. Besides setting out rights and freedoms, it establishes a supervisory mechanism guaranteeing their respect by the states parties. The European Committee of Social Rights is the body responsible for monitoring compliance by the states parties.

Fair balance	The Convention and the Charter (see especially Part V Article G) provide for the limitation of certain rights for the sake of the greater public interest. The European Court of Human Rights has said that when rights are restricted there must be a fair balance between the public interest at stake and the human right in question. The Court is the final arbiter on when this balance has been found. It does however give states a "margin of appreciation" in assessing when the public interest is strong enough to justify restrictions on certain human rights. See also *margin of appreciation; public interest.*
Harmon doctrine	The theory that states have exclusive or sovereign rights over the waters flowing through their territory which they can use regardless of their infringement of the rights of other states.
Home	Article 8 of the Convention guarantees to every individual the enjoyment of his/her home. The right to respect for the home does not only include the right to the actual physical area, but also to the quiet enjoyment of this area. The Court has not limited the concept of "home" to its traditional interpretation, but has described it with the broad notion of "living space", i.e. the physically defined area, where private and family life develops. For example, the Court has considered that a prison cell fulfils the requirements and comes within the protection of Article 8 (see *Giacomelli v. Italy*).
ILC Articles on the Responsibility of States for Internationally Wrongful Acts	The UN International Law Commission adopted in 2001 59 Draft Articles on the Responsibility of States for Internationally Wrongful Acts which have been subsequently endorsed by the General Assembly (GA Res. 56/84 (2001)). According to the articles every internationally wrongful act of a State entails international responsibility of that State (Article 1). A conduct (act or omission) must constitute a breach of international law and be attributable to a State to engage its responsibility (Article 2). However, exceptionally, acts that are generally internationally wrongful may be justified (Chapter V), for instance in case of consent of the impacted State, self-defence, acts which are considered "counter-measures", force majeure, distress, and necessity.[296]

---

296. The articles were used by the ICJ in the case concerning Pulp Mills on the River Uruguay (*Argentina v. Uruguay*), Judgment of 20 April 2010, ICJ General List 135, available at: www.icj-cij.org/docket/files/135/15877.pdf, paragraph 273. Legal Consequences of the *Construction of a Wall in the Occupied Palestinian Territory*, Advisory opinion of 9 July 2004, ICJ Reports (2004) 136, paragraph 140.

Interference   Any instance where the enjoyment of a right set out in the Convention and Charter is limited. Not every interference will mean that there has been violation of the right in question. An interference may be justified by the restrictions provided for in the Convention itself. Generally for an interference to be justified it must be in accordance with the law, pursue a legitimate aim and be proportionate to that aim. See also *legitimate aim*; *prescribed by law*; *proportionality*.

Johannesburg Declaration   The Johannesburg Declaration is the final document of the 2002 UN Environmental Summit, sometimes also referred to as Rio+10 Conference. The Summit improved the Rio Declaration by including the goal of poverty eradication (Principle 11), referred to the private sector (Principle 24) and stressing its liability (Principle 26).

Legitimate aim   Some rights of the Convention and the Charter can be restricted. However, the measures imposing such restrictions should meet a number of requirements for the Court not to find a violation of the right in question. One of them is that they should be necessary in a democratic society, which means that they should answer a pressing social need and pursue a legitimate aim (see Article 8, 9, 10 and 11 of the Convention and Article G Part V of the Charter). Article 8 of the Convention, for instance, lists the broad categories of aims which can be considered as legitimate to justify an interference with the right to private and family life, including national security, territorial integrity or public safety, the prevention of disorder or crime, the protection of health or morals, the protection of the reputation or rights of others. Despite not being part of this explicit list, the Court found that the protection of the environment can be subsumed under the aim of the protection of the rights of others.[297]

Margin of appreciation   Once it is established that measures imposing restrictions on the Convention/Charter are prescribed by law and are necessary in a democratic society in pursuing a legitimate aim, it has to be examined whether the measures in question are proportionate to this legitimate aim. It is in the context of this examination that the Court has established that the authorities are given a certain scope for discretion, i.e. the "margin of appreciation", in determining the most appropriate measures to take in order to reach the legitimate aim sought. The reason is that national authorities are often better placed to assess matters falling under the Articles concerned. The

297. See especially Part I, Section A: Chapter III. For instance, *Pine Valley Developments Ltd and Others v. Ireland*, Judgment of 9 February 1993, Application No. 12472/87, paragraphs 57-59.

scope of this margin of appreciation varies depending on the issue at stake, but, in environmental cases, the Court has found it to be wide. However, this margin of appreciation should not be seen as absolute and preventing the Court from any critical assessment of the proportionality of the measures concerned. Indeed, it has found a number of violations for instance under Article 8 in cases which concerned pollution.

Natural disaster

The Court has not defined the notion of "natural disaster". However, it has used the concept in distinction to dangerous activities in order to describe the scope of the positive obligations resulting from Articles 2 and 8 which are upon a state to protect individuals. It found that as natural disasters are not man-made and in general beyond a state's control, its obligations are therefore different in this situation. Public authorities are still under the obligation to inform, prevent and mitigate impact of natural disasters, to which the Court also refers to as natural hazard, as far as foreseeable and reasonable.[298]

"No harm" principle

The principle of "no harm" (*sic utere tuo ut alienum non laedas*) is at the core of international environmental law. According to the principle no state may act in a manner which inflicts damages on foreign territory, the population of the territory or foreign property.[299] The International Court of Justice has reaffirmed the application of this principle to the environment in its Advisory Opinion on Nuclear Weapons.[300] Moreover, the Trail Smelter case affirmed the existence of a positive obligation to protect other states (and hence their population) from damage by private companies.[301] The principle has also been included in Principle 2 of the 1992 Rio Declaration and 2001 ILC the Draft Articles on the Prevention of Transboundary Harm from Hazardous Activities.[302]

---

298. See *Budayeva and others v. Russia*, judgment of 20 March 2008, Application No. 15339/02, paragraph 158.
299. However, only serious damages may invoke international state responsibility under public international law.
300. *Advisory Opinion on the Legality of the Threat or Use of Nuclear Weapons*, Advisory opinion of 8 July 1996, ICJ Reports (1996) 226, at paragraph 29
301. *Trail Smelter (USA v. Canada)*, Arbitral Award of 16 April 1938 and 11 March 1941, UN Reports of International Arbitral Awards, Vol. III pp. 1905-1982.
302. ILC Draft Articles on Transboundary Harm, ILC Report (2001) GAOR A/56/10, 66, available at: http://untreaty.un.org/ilc/texts/instruments/english/commentaries/9_7_2001.pdf.

Polluter/user pays principle	The polluter/user pays principle stems from general international law. The essence of the polluter pays principle is that those who generate pollution whether it be air, sea, or other, and waste, should also be responsible for the costs of containment, avoidance or abatement of that pollution, regardless of where it occurs, and the removal and disposal of that waste if it is linked to the actions of the polluter/user. It is, *inter alia*, contained in Principle 16 of the Rio Declaration.
Positive obligations	The Court's case-law in respect of a number of provisions of the Convention states that public authorities should not only refrain from interfering arbitrarily with individuals' rights as protected expressly by the articles of the Convention, they should also take active steps to safeguard them. These additional obligations are usually referred to as positive obligations as the authorities are required to act so as to prevent violations of the rights encompassed in the Convention or punish those responsible. For instance, in *Budayeva and others v. Russia* the Court found that the authorities are responsible under Article 2 of the Convention for implementing a defence and warning infrastructure to prevent the loss of life as result of natural disasters.[303] Considering the European Social Charter it is in fact evident that the majority of its provisions are by their very nature positive obligations, e.g. the obligation to guarantee a healthy working environment.
Possessions (peaceful enjoyment of)	The notion of *possessions* within the meaning of Article 1 of Protocol No. 1 to the Convention is not limited to ownership of physical goods and is independent from the formal classification in domestic law. For instance, social security benefits, clientele or economic interests connected with the running of a shop were treated as "possessions" by the Court. The Court has also stated that Article 1 of Protocol No. 1 applies to present and existing possessions but also to claims in respect of which the applicant can argue that he or she has at least a reasonable and "legitimate expectation" of obtaining effective enjoyment of a property right.
Precautionary principle	The *precautionary principle* takes account of the fact that it is often difficult, if not impossible, to assess the precise impact of human action on the environment and that some actions can cause irreparable harm. It requires that if there is a strong suspicion that a certain activity may have detrimental environmental consequences, it is better to control that activity now rather than to wait for incontrovertible scientific evidence. It has been, *inter alia*, included

---

303. See *Budayeva and others v. Russia*, judgment of 20 March 2008, Application No. 15339/02.

in the Rio Declaration, and it played a role in justifying import restrictions in the WTO regime arguing that products had not been produced in a sustainable manner.

Prevention principle

The *prevention principle* is closely related to the precautionary principle. The prevention principle holds that it is generally cheaper and more efficient to prevent environmental catastrophes than to remedy their consequences. Consequently, when assessing the feasibility of preventive action versus remedial action, in the light of, for example, the interference with civil and political rights, preventive actions should be preferred. The principle has been included *inter alia* in the Basel Convention on the Control of Transboundary Movements of Hazardous Wastes and their Disposal of 1989 and has also served as inspiration for the 1983 EC Environmental Action Programme.

Proportionate measures/ proportionality

By *proportionate measures* the Court means measures taken by the authorities that strike a fair balance between the interests of the community and the interests of an individual. The Court applies this test in the context of its examination of the respect for the right to private and family life (Article 8) as well as the right to property (Article 1 of Protocol No. 1) .

Public authorities

Public authorities should be understood broadly as including both national and local authorities of all government branches carrying out activities of a public nature. They will therefore include municipalities as well as prefects or ministries.

Public interest/ general interest

The terms *public interest* and *general interest* appear in Article 1 of the first Protocol of the Convention (Protection of Property). They have also been used by the Court with reference to other articles to assess whether an *interference* by a public authority with an individual's rights can be justified. An interference may serve a legitimate objective in the *public* or *general interest* even if it does not benefit the community as a whole, but advances the *public interest* by benefiting a section of the community.[304]

Public participation principle

The principle is at the core of the Aarhus convention. In general, it requires states to take the public into account and offer procedural means to have its concerns voiced and considered.

---

304. See *James and Others v. the United Kingdom*, Judgment of 21 February 1986, paragraphs 39-46.

Rio Declaration	The Rio Declaration on Environment and Development[305] concluded the 1992 United Nations "Conference on Environment and Development". The Rio Declaration consists of 27 principles intended to guide future sustainable development around the world. The declaration stresses the principle of sustainable development (Principles 4 and 8), the precautionary and preventive principle (Principle 15), the polluter/user-pays principle (Principle 16), the principle of common but differentiated responsibilities (Principle 7), and the right to the exploitation of one's own resources save the absence of harm of ones neighbours (Principle 2). It also mentions the right to development (Principle 3).
Stockholm Declaration	The Stockholm Declaration[306] is the final document of the United Nations Conference on the Human Environment in 1972 – the first UN conference on the environment. A right to a healthy environment is proclaimed in the declaration for the first time.
Subsidiarity (principle of)	The *principle of subsidiarity* is one the founding principles of the human rights protection mechanism of the Convention. According to this principle it should first and foremost be for national authorities to ensure that the rights enshrined in the Convention are not violated and to offer redress if ever they are. The Convention mechanism and the European Court of Human Rights should only be a last resort in cases where the national level has not offered the protection or redress needed.
Sustainable development principle	This principle holds that development must be capable of being maintained in the long term and that sustainable production should be favoured when possible. This principle can be seen as having an economic, environmental, and ecological dimension, which must be balanced (See Principles 4 and 8 of the Rio Declaration).
United Nations Framework Convention on Climate Change (UNFCCC)	The UNFCCC is a result of the 1992 United Nations Conference on Environment and Development in Rio. The objective of the treaty is to establish a framework to consider what can be done to reduce global warming and to cope with whatever temperature increases are inevitable. A number of nations approved, in addition to the treaty, the Kyoto Protocol of 1997, which has more powerful (and legally binding) measures for regulating, *inter alia*, CO_2 emissions.

305. Adopted on 14 June 1992, available at:
    www.unep.org/Documents.Multilingual/Default.asp?documentid=78&articleid=1163.
306. Adopted on 16 June 1972, available at:
    www.unep.org/Documents.Multilingual/Default.asp?documentid=97&articleid=1503.

Appendix II: Judgments and decisions of the European Court of Human Rights relevant to the environment

	Decision on admissibility or Judgment	Date	2	3	6 (1)	13	8	10	11	1-P1
*Arrondelle v. United Kingdom**	Admissible (friendly settlement)	15/7/1980				□	□			□
Zimmerman and Steiner v. Switzerland	Judgment	13/7/1983			■					
*G. and E. v. Norway**	Inadmissible	3/10/1983				□	□	□		□
*Baggs v. United Kingdom**	Partially admissible	16/10/1985			□	□	□			□
*Rayner v. United Kingdom**	Partially admissible	16/7/1986			□		□			□
*Vearnacombe and others v. United Kingdom**	Admissible	18/1/1989			□	□	□			□
Powell and Rayner v. United Kingdom	Judgment	21/2/1990			□	□	□			
*S. v. France**	Inadmissible	17/5/1990						□		□

* = Commission Decision | GC = Grand Chamber
□ = Articles invoked | ■ = Violation

Case	Type	Date							
Fredin v. Sweden	Judgment	18/2/1991	■						□
Pine Valley Development Ltd v. Ireland	Judgment	29/11/1991		□					□
Zander v. Sweden	Judgment	25/11/1993	■						
López Ostra v. Spain	Judgment	9/12/1994	□				■		
Piermont v. France	Judgment	27/4/1995					■		
Matos e Silva Lda. and others v. Portugal	Judgment	16/9/1996	■	□					■
Buckley v. United Kingdom	Judgment	25/9/1996				□			
Balmer-Schafroth and others v. Switzerland	Judgment (GC)	26/8/1997		□	□				
Guerra and others v. Italy	Judgment (GC)	19/2/1998	□				■	□	
McGinley and Egan v. United Kingdom	Judgment	9/6/1998		□	□	□			
L.C.B. v. United Kingdom	Judgment	9/6/1998	□	□		□	□		
Hertel v. Switzerland	Judgment	25/8/1998		□			□	■	
Steel and others v. United Kingdom	Judgment	23/9/1998				□			
Chassagnou and others v. France	Judgment (GC)	29/4/1999						■	■
L'Association des Amis de St-Raphaël et Fréjus and others v. France	Inadmissible	29/2/2000		□	□				□
Athanassoglou and others v. Switzerland	Judgment (GC)	6/4/2000		□	□				
Pagliccia and others v. Italy	Inadmissible	7/9/2000				□			
Ünver v. Turkey	Inadmissible	26/9/2000		□					□
Sciavilla v. Italy	Inadmissible	14/11/2000				□			

* = Commission Decision | GC = Grand Chamber
□ = Articles invoked | ■ = Violation

Chapman v. United Kingdom	Judgment (GC)	18/1/2001		□		□			□
Jane Smith v. United Kingdom	Judgment (GC)	18/1/2001		□		□			□
Coster v. United Kingdom	Judgment (GC)	18/1/2001			□				□
Thoma v. Luxembourg	Judgment	29/3/2001					■		
Dati v. Italy	Inadmissible	22/1/2002			□				
Burdov v. Russia	Judgment	7/5/2002		■					■
Demuth v. Switzerland	Judgment	15/11/2002					□		
Dactylidi v. Greece	Judgment	27/3/2003		■	■				
Papastavrou and others v. Greece	Judgment	10/4/2003							□
Kyrtatos v. Greece	Judgment	22/5/2003		■	□				
Hatton and others v. United Kingdom	Judgment (GC)	8/7/2003				■	□		
Lam and others v. United Kingdom	Inadmissible	8/7/2003	□		□	□	□		□
Fadeyeva v. Russia	Partially admissible	16/10/2003	□	□	□		□		
Ashworth and others v. United Kingdom	Inadmissible	20/1/2004				□	□		□
Taşkın and others v. Turkey	Partially admissible	29/1/2004	□		□	□	□		□
Gorraiz Lizarraga v. Spain	Judgment	27/4/2004			□		□		□
Aparicio Benito v. Spain	Partly inadmissible and adjourned	4/5/2004	□			□	□		
Vides Aizsardzibas Klubs v. Latvia	Judgment	27/5/2004						■	
Ledyayeva v. Russia	Partially admissible	16/9/2004	□	□	□		□	□	
Kapsalis et Nima-Kapsali v. Greece	Inadmissible	23/9/2004			□	□			□

Case	Type	Date						
Giani v. Italy	Inadmissible	28/10/2004	□		□	□		
Balzarini and others v. Italy	Inadmissible	28/10/2004			□	□		
Ward v. United Kingdom	Inadmissible	9/11/2004	□			□		
Taşkın and others v. Turkey	Judgment	10/11/2004	□	■	□	■		
Moreno Gómez v. Spain	Judgment	16/11/2004				■		
Öneryıldız v. Turkey	Judgment (GC)	30/11/2004	■		■	□		■
Botti v. Italy	Inadmissible	2/12/2004	□			□		
Steel and Morris v. United Kingdom	Judgment	15/2/2005		■			■	
Fadeyeva v. Russia	Judgment	9/6/2005				■		
Okyay and Others v. Turkey	Judgment	12/7/2005		■				
N.A. and Others v. Turkey	Judgment	11/10/2005						■
Roche v. United Kingdom	Judgment (GC)	19/10/2005	□	□	■	□		□
Luginbühl v. Switzerland	Inadmissible	17/1/2006	□			□		
Valico S. R. L. v. Italy	Inadmissible	21/03/2006		□				□
Öckan and others v. Turkey	Judgment	28/3/2006	□	■	□	■		
Ledyayeva and Others v. Russia	Judgment	26/10/2006				■		
Giacomelli v. Italy	Judgment	2/11/2006				■		
Aparicio Benito v. Spain (French only)	Inadmissible	13/11/2006	□			□		
Murillo Saldias v. Spain	Inadmissible	28/11/2006	□		□	□		
Lemke v. Turkey	Judgment	7/6/2007	□	■	□	■		
Verein gegen Tierfabriken v. Switzerland	Judgment	4/10/2007	□				■	

* = Commission Decision | GC = Grand Chamber
□ = Articles invoked | ■ = Violation

Case	Decision	Date					
Hamer v. Belgium (French only)	Judgment	27/11/2007		■	□		□
Z.A.N.T.E. – Marathonisi A.E. v. Greece	Judgment	6/12/2007					■
Budayeva and Others v. Russia	Judgment	22/3/2008	■		□		□
Borysiewicz v. Poland	Judgment	1/7/2008		■	□		
Turgut v. Turkey	Judgment	8/7/2008					■
Mangouras v. Spain	Judgment	8/1/2009	No violation of Article 5				
Stoine Hristov v. Bulgaria (French only)	Judgment	16/01/2009				□	
Tătar v. Romania	Judgment	27/1/2009				■	
Satir v. Turkey	Judgment	10/3/2009	□				■
Brânduşe v. Romania	Judgment	7/4/2009	■			■	
Verein gegen Tierfabriken v. Switzerland (No. 2)	Judgment (GC)	30/6/2009				■	
Leon and Agnieszka Kania v. Poland	Judgment	21/7/2009		■	□	□	
Depalle v. France	Judgment (GC)	29/3/2010					□
Brosset-Triboulet and Others v. France	Judgment (GC)	29/3/2010					□
Băcilă v. Romania (French only)	Judgment	30/3/2010				■	
Mangouras v. Spain	Judgment (GC)	28/9/2010	No violation of Article 5				
Deés v. Hungary	Judgment	9/11/2010		■	■		
Dubetska and Others v. Urkaine	Judgment	10/2/2011				■	
Ioan Marchiş and Others v. Romania	Inadmissible	28/6/2011			□		
Grimkovskaya v. Ukraine	Judgment	21/7/2011		□	■		

Appendix III: Reference to other instruments relevant to the environment in ECHR case-law

The Court in its case-law has often made reference to international environmental law standards and principles.

For instance, a core principle referred to by the Court is *sic utere tuo ut alienum non laedas* (principle of "no harm"),[307] which has replaced the doctrine of absolute sovereignty.[308] According to this principle no State may act in a manner which inflicts damages on foreign territory, the population of the territory or foreign property. The International Court of Justice has reaffirmed its application in the realm of the environment in its Advisory Opinion on Nuclear Weapons.[309]

Moreover, the Trail Smelter case affirmed the existence of a positive obligation to protect other States (and hence their population) from damage inflicted by private companies.[310] This also appears in Principle 2 of the 1992 Rio Declaration[311] and in the 2001 ILC Draft Articles on the Prevention of Transboundary Harm from Hazardous Activities.[312]

---

307. See also Appendix 1 "Glossary".
308. Also known with respect to environmental matters as "Harmon-Doctrine".
309. *Legality of the Threat or Use of Nuclear Weapons*, Advisory opinion of 8 July 1996, ICJ Reports (1996) 226, paragraph 29.
310. Trail Smelter (*USA v. Canada*), arbitral award of 16 April 1938 and 11 March 1941, UN Reports of International Arbitral Awards, Vol. III, pp. 1905-1982.

The Court mentioned in *Tătar v. Romania* Principles 2 and 14 of the Rio Declaration under the list of relevant law. More importantly, it held in paragraph 111-112, as part of its reasoning: *"Concernant ce dernier aspect, la Cour rappelle, dans l'esprit des principes n° 21 de la Déclaration de Stockholm et n° 14 de la Déclaration de Rio, le devoir général des autorités de décourager et prévenir les transferts dans d'autres Etats de substances qui provoquent une grave détérioration de l'environnement [...]. La Cour observe également qu'au-delà du cadre législatif national instauré par la loi sur la protection de l'environ-nement, des normes internationales spécifiques existaient, qui auraient pu être appliquées par les autorités roumaines."* In the same case the Court referred in paragraphs 69 and 120 to the related "precautionary principle"

To mention another example, the "polluter pays" principle,[313] con-tained e.g. in the Rio Declaration, holds that the polluter should in principle bear the cost of pollution regardless of where it occurs. The Court included in a number of cases[314] in the list of relevant law the EU directive 2004/35/EC, which aims to establish a framework of environmental liability based on the "polluter pays" principle, with a view to preventing and remedying environmental damage. Moreover, in *Öneryıldız v. Turkey* it referred to the Convention on Civil Liability for Damage resulting from Activities Dangerous to the Environment, whose provision are an elaboration of the prin-ciple.

Judgments of the European Court of Human Rights which refer explicitly to other international environmental protection instru-ments are displayed in chronological order hereafter, with the relevant extracts. [...]

---

311. Rio Declaration on Environment and Development, United Nations Conference on Environ-ment and Development, 14 June 1992, available at: www.unep.org/Documents.Multilingual/ Default.asp?documentid=78&articleid=1163, also Stockholm Declaration Principle 21, 16 June 1972, available at:
www.unep.org/Documents.Multilingual/Default.asp?documentid=97&articleid=1503 .
312. ILC Draft Articles on Transboundary Harm, ILC Report (2001) GAOR A/56/10, 66, available at:http://untreaty.un.org/ilc/texts/instruments/english/commentaries/9_7_2001.pdf .
313. See also Appendix 1 "Glossary".
314. e.g. *Tătar v. Romania*, judgment of 27.01.2009 and *Mangouras v. Spain*, judgment of 08.01.2009

Case	Reference to	Quotation/Comment
Guerra and Others v. Italy	**PACE resolution**	"Of particular relevance among the various Council of Europe documents in the field under consideration in the present case is Parliamentary Assembly Resolution 1087 (1996) on the consequences of the Chernobyl disaster, which was adopted on 26 April 1996 (at the 16th Sitting). Referring not only to the risks associated with the production and use of nuclear energy in the civil sector but also to other matters, it states "public access to clear and full information ... must be viewed as a basic human right"." (List of relevant Council of Europe text)
Kyratatos v. Greece	**International instruments**	"Neither Article 8 nor any of the other Articles of the Convention are specifically designed to provide general protection of the environment as such; to that effect, other international instruments and domestic legislation are more pertinent in dealing with this particular aspect."
Taşkın and others v. Turkey	**Rio Declaration**	(List of relevant law)
Taşkın and others v. Turkey	**Aarhus Convention**	(List of relevant law)
Taşkın and others v. Turkey	**PACE recommendation**	Recommendation 1614 (2003) on Environment and Human Rights (List of relevant law)
Öneryıldız v. Turkey	**PACE resolution**	Resolution 587 (1975) on problems connected with the disposal of urban and industrial waste, Resolution 1087 (1996) on the consequences of the Chernobyl disaster, Recommendation 1225 (1993) on the management, treatment, recycling and marketing of waste (List of relevant Council of Europe text)
Öneryıldız v. Turkey (GC)	**Committee of Ministers recommendation**	Recommendation No. R (96) 12 on the distribution of powers and responsibilities between central authorities and local and regional authorities with regard to the environment. (List of relevant Council of Europe text)

Case	Reference to	Quotation/Comment
Öneryıldız v. Turkey (GC)	Convention on Civil Liability for Damage resulting from Activities Dangerous to the Environment (ETS No 152)	(List of relevant Council of Europe text)
Öneryıldız v. Turkey (GC)	Convention on the Protection of the Environment through Criminal Law (ETSNo. 172)	(List of relevant Council of Europe text)
Öneryıldız v. Turkey (GC)	European standards	"It can be seen from these documents that primary responsibility for the treatment of household waste rests with local authorities, which the governments are obliged to provide with financial and technical assistance. The operation by the public authorities of a site for the permanent deposit of waste is described as a "dangerous activity", and "loss of life" resulting from the deposit of waste at such a site is considered to be "damage" incurring the liability of the public authorities."
Öneryıldız v. Turkey (GC)	Convention on the Protection of the Environment through Criminal Law (ETS No. 172)	"In that connection, the Strasbourg Convention calls on the Parties to adopt such measures" as may be necessary to establish as criminal offences" acts involving the "disposal, treatment, storage ... of hazardous waste which causes or is likely to cause death or serious injury to any person ...", and provides that such offences may also be committed "with negligence" (Articles 2 to 4). Although this instrument has not yet come into force, it is very much in keeping with the current trend towards harsher penalties for damage to the environment, an issue inextricably linked with the endangering of human life. [...] Article 6 of the Strasbourg Convention also requires the adoption of such measures as may be necessary to make these offences punishable by criminal sanctions which take into account the serious nature of the offences; these must include imprisonment of the perpetrators."
Öneryıldız v. Turkey (GC)	European standards	Where such dangerous activities are concerned, public access to clear and full information is viewed as a basic human right; for example, the above-mentioned Resolution 1087 (1996) makes clear that this right must not be taken to be limited to the risks associated with the use of nuclear energy in the civil sector."

Case	Reference to	Quotation/Comment
Öneryıldız v. Turkey (GC)	**European standards**	"Referring to the examples provided by cases such as [...] and to the European standards in this area, the Chamber emphasised that the protection of the right to life, as required by Article 2 of the Convention, could be relied on in connection with the operation of waste-collection sites, on account of the potential risks inherent in that activity."
Öneryıldız v. Turkey (GC)	**European standards**	"The Court considers that this obligation must be construed as applying in the context of any activity, whether public or not, in which the right to life may be at stake, and a fortiori in the case of industrial activities, which by their very nature are dangerous, such as the operation of waste-collection sites ("dangerous activities" – for the relevant European standards, see paragraphs 59-60 above)."
Okay and Others v. Turkey	**Rio Declaration**	(List of relevant law)
Okay and Others v. Turkey	**PACE recommendation**	Recommendation 1614 (2003) on Environment and Human Rights (List of relevant law)
Borysiewicz v. Poland	**International environmental standards**	"[T]he Court notes that the applicant has not submitted [...] noise tests which would have allowed the noise levels in her house to be ascertained, and for it to be determined whether they exceeded the norms set either by domestic law or by applicable international environmental standards, or exceeded the environmental hazards inherent in life in every modern town."
Demir and Bayakara v. Turkey	**Aarhus Convention**	"In the *Taşkın and Others v. Turkey* case, the Court built on its case-law concerning Article 8 of the Convention in matters of environmental protection (an aspect regarded as forming part of the individual's private life) largely on the basis of principles enshrined in the Aarhus Convention on Access to Information, Public Participation in Decision-making and Access to Justice in Environmental Matters (ECE/CEP/43) (see *Taşkın and Others v. Turkey*, No. 49517/99, §§ 99 and 119, 4 December 2003). Turkey had not signed the Aarhus Convention."
Mangouras v. Spain	**International Convention for the Prevention of Pollution from Ships**	(List of relevant law)
Mangouras v. Spain	**United Nations Convention on the Law of the Sea**	(List of relevant law)

Case	Reference to	Quotation/Comment
Mangouras v. Spain	EC directive	Directive 2004/35/CE of the European Parliament and of the Council of 21 April 2004 on environmental liability with regard to the prevention and remedying of environmental damage (List of relevant law)
Mangouras v. Spain	EC directive	Directive 2005/35/EC of the European Parliament and of the Council of 7 September 2005 on ship-source pollution and on the introduction of penalties for infringements (List of relevant law)
Tătar v. Romania	EC directive	Directive No. 2004/35/CE (List of relevant law)
Tătar v. Romania	Stockholm Declaration	(List of relevant law)
Tătar v. Romania	Rio Declaration	(List of relevant law)
Tătar v. Romania	Aarhus Convention	(List of relevant law)
Tătar v. Romania	ICJ judgment	*Gabcikovo Nagymaros (Hungary v. Slovakia)* (List of relevant law)
Tătar v. Romania	PACE resolution	Resolution 1430 (2005) on Industrial hazards (List of relevant law)
Tătar v. Romania	EU directive	Directives 2006/21/CE and 2004/35/CE on environmental liability with regard to the prevention and remedying of environmental damage (List of relevant law)
Tătar v. Romania	EU Commission Communication	COM/2000/0664 final on security of mining activities (List of relevant law)

Case	Reference to	Quotation/Comment
Tătar v. Romania	**Precautionary principle (ECJ, Maastricht, Amsterdam Treaty)**	« En vertu du principe de précaution, l'absence de certitude compte tenu des connaissances scientifiques et techniques du moment ne saurait justifier que l'Etat retarde l'adoption de mesures effectives et proportionnées visant à prévenir un risque de dommages graves et irréversibles à l'environnement. Dans l'histoire de la construction européenne, le principe de précaution a été introduit par le Traité de Maastricht […]. Cette étape marque, au niveau européen, l'évolution du principe d'une conception philosophique vers une norme juridique. Les lignes directrices du principe ont été fixées par la Commission européenne dans sa communication du 2 février 2000 sur le recours au principe de précaution. La jurisprudence communautaire a fait application de ce principe dans des affaires concernant surtout la santé, alors que le traité n'énonce le principe qu'en ce qui concerne la politique de la Communauté dans le domaine de l'environnement. La Cour de justice des Communautés européennes ("CJCE") considère ce principe, à la lumière de l'article 17 § 2, 1er alinéa, CE, comme l'un des fondements de la politique de protection d'un niveau élevé poursuivie par la Communauté dans le domaine de l'environnement. Selon la jurisprudence de la CJCE, lorsque "des incertitudes subsistent quant à l'existence où à la portée des risques pour la santé des personnes, les institutions peuvent prendre des mesures sans avoir à attendre que la réalité et la gravité ce ces risques soient pleinement démontrées" [Royaume Uni/Commission, Aff C-180/96, et CJCE, National Farmer's Union, C-157/96,] » (French only)
Tătar v. Romania	**UN and EU reports**	« La Cour observe qu'au moins pendant un certain laps de temps après l'accident écologique de janvier 2000 différents éléments polluants (cyanures, plomb, zinc, cadmium) dépassant les normes internes et internationales admises ont été présents dans l'environnement, notamment à proximité de l'habitation des requérants. C'est ce que confirment les conclusions des rapports officiels établis après l'accident par les Nations unies (UNEP/OCHA), l'Union européenne (Task Force) et le ministère roumain de l'Environnement (voir les paragraphes 26, 28 et 63 ci-dessus).La Cour ne voit aucune raison de douter de la sincérité des observations formulées par les requérants à cet égard. » (French only)

Case	Reference to	Quotation/Comment
Tătar *v. Romania*	**Rio Declaration**	« Concernant ce dernier aspect, la Cour rappelle, dans l'esprit des principes nº 21 de la Déclaration de Stockholm et nº 14 de la Déclaration de Rio, le devoir général des autorités de décourager et prévenir les transferts dans d'autres Etats de substances qui provoquent une grave détérioration de l'environnement (voir pp. 21 et 23 ci-dessus).La Cour observe également qu'au-delà du cadre législatif national instauré par la loi sur la protection de l'environnement, des normes internationales spécifiques existaient, qui auraient pu être appliquées par les autorités roumaines » (French only)
Tătar *v. Romania*	**Stockholm Declaration**	« Concernant ce dernier aspect, la Cour rappelle, dans l'esprit des principes nº 21 de la Déclaration de Stockholm et nº 14 de la Déclaration de Rio, le devoir général des autorités de décourager et prévenir les transferts dans d'autres Etats de substances qui provoquent une grave détérioration de l'environnement (voir pp. 21 et 23 ci-dessus).La Cour observe également qu'au-delà du cadre législatif national instauré par la loi sur la protection de l'environnement, des normes internationales spécifiques existaient, qui auraient pu être appliquées par les autorités roumaines » (French only)
Tătar *v. Romania*	**Aarhus Convention**	« Au niveau international, la Cour rappelle que l'accès à l'information, la participation du public au processus décisionnel et l'accès à la justice en matière d'environnement sont consacrés par la Convention d'Aarhus du 25 juin 1998, ratifiée par la Roumanie le 22 mai 2000 (voir p. 23, c). Dans le même sens, la Résolution no 1430/2005 de l'Assemblée parlementaire du Conseil de l'Europe sur les risques industriels renforce, entre autres, le devoir pour les États membres d'améliorer la diffusion d'informations dans ce domaine (voir p. 25, f). » (French only)
Tătar *v. Romania*	**Precautionary principle**	"… appeared for the first time in the Rio declaration"
Brosset- *Triboulet and* *Others* *v. France (GC)*	**Committee of Ministers recommendation**	Recommendation No. R (97) 9 of the Committee of Ministers on a policy for the development of sustainable environment-friendly tourism (List of relevant law)
Brosset- *Triboulet and* *Others* *v. France (GC)*	**European Code of Conduct for Coastal Zones**	(List of relevant law)

Case	Reference to	Quotation/Comment
Depalle v. France (GC)	**Committee of Ministers recommendation**	Recommendation No. R (97) 9 of the Committee of Ministers on a policy for the development of sustainable environment-friendly tourism (List of relevant law)
Depalle v. France (GC)	**European Code of Conduct for Coastal Zones**	(List of relevant law)
Mangouras v. Spain (GC)	**EC directive**	Directive 2005/35/EC on ship-source pollution (List of relevant law)
Mangouras v. Spain (GC)	**ECJ judgment**	Case C-308/06 on validity of Directive 2004/35/EC (List of relevant law)
Mangouras v. Spain (GC)	**United Nations Convention on the Law of the Sea**	(List of relevant law)
Mangouras v. Spain (GC)	**ITLOS case-law**	(List of relevant law)
Mangouras v. Spain (GC)	**International Convention for the Prevention of Pollution from Ships**	(List of relevant law)
Mangouras v. Spain (GC)	**International Convention on Civil Liability for Oil Pollution Damage**	(List of relevant law)
Mangouras v. Spain (GC)	**The London P&I Rules**	(List of relevant law)
Mangouras v. Spain (GC)	**European and international law**	"[T]he Court cannot overlook the growing and legitimate concern both in Europe and internationally in relation to environmental offences. This is demonstrated in particular by States' powers and obligations regarding the prevention of maritime pollution and by the unanimous determination of States and European and international organisations to identify those responsible, ensure that they appear for trial and, if appropriate, impose sanctions on them (see "Relevant domestic and international law" above). A tendency can also be observed to use criminal law as a means of enforcing the environmental obligations imposed by European and international law. The Court considers that these new realities have to be taken into account in interpreting the requirements of Article 5§3 in this regard. It takes the view that the increasingly high standard being required in the area of the protection of human rights and fundamental liberties correspondingly and inevitably requires greater firmness in assessing breaches of the fundamental values of democratic societies. [...]"

Case	Reference to	Quotation/Comment
Mangouras v. Spain (GC)	ITLOS case-law	"It takes the view that the increasingly high standard being required in the area of the protection of human rights and fundamental liberties correspondingly and inevitably requires greater firmness in assessing breaches of the fundamental values of democratic societies."
Grimkovskaya v. Ukraine	Aarhus Convention	(List of relevant law)
Grimkovskaya v. Ukraine	PACE recommendation	Recommendation 1614 (2003) of 27 June 2003 on environment and human rights (List of relevant law)
Grimkovskaya v. Ukraine	Aarhus Convention	"[The Court] also notes that as of 30 October 2001 the Aarhus Convention, which concerns access to information, participation of the public in decision-making and access to justice in environmental matters has entered into force in respect of Ukraine."
Grimkovskaya v. Ukraine	Aarhus Convention	"72. Overall, the Court attaches importance to the following factors. First, the Government's failure to show that the decision [...] was preceded by an adequate environmental feasibility study and followed by the enactment of a reasonable environmental management policy. Second, the Government did not show that the applicant had a meaningful opportunity to contribute to the related decision-making processes, including by challenging the municipal policies before an independent authority. Bearing those two factors and the Aarhus Convention [...] in mind, the Court cannot conclude that a fair balance was struck in the present case."

Appendix IV: Good practices

The following represents a selection of practical initiatives and legal frameworks aimed at protecting the environment and respecting the obligations stemming from the European Convention on Human Rights and the European Social Charter. The examples have been taken from the responses provided by a number of member states in 2010 and 2011.[315] The examples do not represent an exhaustive list but rather serve to illustrate some typical actions of member states.

This summary of good practices has been broken down into five categories:

1. Embedding environmental rights in the national policy and legal framework

2. Establishing control over potentially harmful environmental activities

3. Requiring environmental impact assessments (EIAs)

4. Securing public participation and access to information on environmental matters

5. Making environmental rights judiciable and the environment a public concern.

---

315. See compilation of contributions from member states – documents GT-DEV-ENV(2011)03, GT-DEV-ENV(2011)03_Add1 and GT-DEV-ENV(2011)03_Add2.

1. Embedding environmental rights in the national policy and legal framework

A. Environment and national constitutions

In several countries the environment is protected through the constitution. For example, the **Bulgarian** Constitution provides for the right to a "healthy and favourable environment in accordance with the established standards and norms" (Article 55). The same article proclaims vice-versa an obligation for the citizens to protect the environment.

The Constitution of **Poland** also contains several environmental provisions. Article 74 requires public authorities to pursue policies which ensure the ecological security of current and future generations. Article 68, paragraph 4, places an explicit duty on public authorities to prevent negative health consequences resulting from the degradation of the environment.

Article 44 of the Constitution of the **Slovak Republic** provides explicitly that "everyone shall have the right to a favourable environment". It places a duty on everyone to protect and improve the environment. Likewise, Article 74 of the **Serbian** Constitution places an obligation to preserve and improve the environment for "everyone" in addition to prescribing the right to a healthy environment. The Constitution of **Slovenia** also contains a "right to a healthy living environment" (Article 72).

The Constitution of the Republic of **Albania** stipulates that the state shall aim at ensuring "a healthy and ecologically sustainable environment for current and future generations" as well "as rational exploitation of forests, water, pastures, and other natural resources on the basis of a sustainable development principle" (Article 59).

On the basis of a special federal constitutional Act, **Austria** commits itself to comprehensive protection of the environment, i.e. to protecting the natural environment as the basis of mankind's life against detrimental effects. Due to that constitutional commitment, the legislative and administrative organs are required to improve environmental protection. In its case-law, the Austrian Constitutional Court has given a broad meaning to the notion of "environmental protection" as employed in the Act.

While the **Czech** Constitution provides only a general provision on environmental protection (Article 7), the Czech Charter of Fundamental Rights and Freedoms, which is part of the constitutional legislation, grants the "right to a favourable living environment" as well as "the right to timely and complete information about the state of the living environment and natural resources" (Article 35). In exercising his/her rights nobody may endanger or cause damage to the living environment, natural resources, the wealth of natural species, and cultural monuments beyond limits set by law.

Mindful of its responsibility toward future generations, the Basic Law for the Federal Republic of **Germany** imposes an obligation on the state to protect the natural foundations of life and animals by legislation and, in accordance with law and justice, by executive and judicial action, all within the framework of the constitutional order (Article 20a).

The Spanish Constitution sets out that everyone has the right to enjoy an environment suitable for the development of the person, as well as the duty to preserve it (Article 45). The public authorities shall safeguard rational use of all natural resources with a view to protecting and improving the quality of life and preserving and restoring the environment, by relying on essential collective solidarity.

The **Swedish** Constitution guarantees that the public institutions shall promote sustainable development leading to a good environment for present and future generations (Chapter 1, Article 2).

Switzerland's Constitution has several provisions relating to environmental protection. While Article 73 of the Swiss Constitution enshrines the principle of sustainable development, Article 74 deals more specifically with environmental protection. Articles 76 to 79 treat the handling of water, forests, the protection of natural and cultural heritage and fishing and hunting.

However, the fact that the constitution of a country does not contain any specific article on the environment does not mean that the protection cannot be claimed through other constitutional provisions. For instance, in **Cyprus** claims for the protection of the environment have been made through the constitutional provisions on human rights (right to life and corporal integrity, prohibition of inhuman and degrading treatment, rights to respect for private and family life, right to property).

B. Environment and national legislation

Most countries have developed either framework legislation often defining basic principles of environmental protection and/or they have enacted a number of specific legislations in the main environmental sectors.

Examples of countries with framework legislation on the environment

Albania passed the Law on Environmental Protection in 2002. In addition there are other specialised legislation which regulate, for instance, the treatment of dangerous wastes, ionising radiation, gathering of statistical data on the environment, strategic environmental assessments, air and water quality, waste management, environmental impact assessments, chemicals and hazardous waste, biodiversity, fauna protection, including Integrated Pollution Prevention and Control, Large Combustion Plant, Seveso II, Pollution Release and Transfer Register and the Liability Directive.

In **Bulgaria** the horizontal legislation in the field of environment conservation includes the Environmental Protection Act, Liability for Prevention and Remedying of Environmental Damage Act, and the Access to Public Information Act. In addition, separate legal acts have been passed in main sectors such as on air quality, waste management, water quality, nature conservation, chemicals and mine waste.

The **Czech Republic** has enacted the Law on the Environment. The horizontal legislation sets rules in particular for access to environmental information, environmental impact assessment, urban planning, integrated pollution prevention and control, environmental damage, prevention and remedies and environmental criminal offences. The sectoral environmental legislation covers a wide range of environmental issues, specifically water, soil, air and ozone protection, nature protection, waste management, forest management, use of mineral resources, chemicals management, prevention of industrial accidents, the use of genetically modified organisms, climate change, and the use of nuclear energy, radiation protection and protection against noise.

Hungary established the Act on the General Rules of Environmental Protection.

Norway has adopted the Nature Diversity Act.

Poland has enacted the Nature Protection Act and the Environmental Protection Law. In addition, there are also specialised environmental legislations which regulate, among other things, the issue of waste, genetically modified organisms, the use of atomic energy, the emission of greenhouse gases and other substances, water protection, carrying out geological work and extracting mineral deposits, and forest protection.

Slovenia has adopted the Environment Protection Act of 2004. Based on this act further regulations relating to air quality, waste management, nature protection, soil protection and noise protection have been enacted.

Sweden adopted the Environmental Code in 1999. At the same time a system of environmental courts was introduced. The court system presently consists of five regional environmental courts and one Environmental Court of Appeal.

Examples of countries with a number of specific legislations on the environment

In **Austria** provisions on the protection of the environment are found for example in the Trade Code, the Water Act, the Waste Management Act, the Air Pollution Law for Boiler Facilities, the Forestry Act and the Air Pollution Impact Act.

Cyprus has enacted a multitude of sector and problem specific legislation concerning, *inter alia,* ambient air and water quality, air and ground water protection against pollution, industrial pollution and risk management, management waste and chemicals, disposal of hazardous and toxic waste, polluting substances, animal waste, biotechnology, nature protection, noise, radiation protection, consumer protection, permissible sound levels, exhaust fumes, emissions of pollutants, chemicals, genetically modified products, energy conservation, renewable energy sources and climate change.

In 2005 **Estonia** passed the Environmental Assessment and the Environmental Management System Act.

Serbia has enacted specific legislation to regulate planning and construction, mining, geological research, waters, land, forest plants and animals, national parks, fisheries, hunting, waste management, protection against ionic radiation and nuclear safety. In 2004, Serbia enacted the Law on Environmental Protection, Law on Strategic Environmental Assessment, Law on Environmental Impact Assessment and Law on Integrated Pollution Prevention and Control to harmonise its framework with EU regulations. The Criminal Code includes a special chapter on offences against the environment. The initiative to amend the Criminal Code in order to fully comply with Directive 2008/99/EC (crime in the area of environment) was initiated by the Ministry of Environment, Mining and Spatial Planning and approved by the Ministry of Justice. In the course of 2009 and 2010 a new set of laws and implementing legislation in the area of environmental protection was adopted, notably on chemicals, noise protection, prohibition of development, production, storage and usage of chemical weapons, waste, package and packaging waste and biocide products, air protection, nature protection, protection against non-ionising radiation, protection against ionising radiation and sustainable use of fish stock.

The **Slovak Republic** has enacted multitudinous and multifarious environmental legislation in the areas of public administration, environmental funding, examination of influence over the environment, prevention of serious industrial accidents, environmental designation of products, environmental management and auditing, integrated prevention and control of environmental pollution, protection of land and nature, genetically modified organisms, water economy, protection of the quality and quantity of water, protection of ambient air and ozone layer, waste economy, geological works and environmental damages. Offences committed against the environment are defined in the Criminal Code.

In **Spain,** the national Parliament has enacted a specific legislation on natural heritage and biodiversity, assessment of the effects of certain plans and programmes, coastal areas, continental water, the national parks network, environmental liability, integrated pollution prevention and control, the quality and protection of the air, waste and waste packaging, environmental noise, geological sequestration of CO_2, access to information and public participation on environmental matters. The regions may establish a higher level of protection to the basic legislation, but not a lower one.

Switzerland has enacted multiple laws of which the most important one is the Environmental Protection Act, which deals with, *inter alia*, pollution control (air pollution, noise, vibrations and radiation), environmental impact assessment, environmentally hazardous substances, the handling of organisms, waste and the remediation of polluted sites. Other crucial laws are the Federal Act on the Protection of Nature and Cultural Heritage, the Water Protection Act, the Forest Act and newly the Federal Act on the Reduction of CO_2 Emissions.

C. Environment and national policy frameworks including plans of actions and institutional arrangements

Cyprus has drawn up and implemented several action plans for the promotion of environmental matters, green and eco label policies, and green public procurement. Responsibility for the protection of the environment is allocated to different ministries. The Ministry of Agriculture, Natural Resources and Environment, namely its Environment Service, is vested with the overall responsibility and the implementation of environmental legislation and programmes.

However other ministries also share responsibility in this area, such as the Ministry of Interior, the Ministry of Labour and Social Insurance, the Ministry of Health and the Ministry of Commerce and Industry.

Hungary has established a "Green-Point Service" as part of the Public Relations Office, which works within the framework of the Ministry for Environment and Water. The service provides, *inter alia*, access to environmental information and operates a nationwide information network of environment, nature and water protection.

In **Slovenia**, the Resolution on the National Environmental Protection Programme has established four areas which are of high policy concern: climate change, nature and biodiversity, quality of life, and waste and industrial pollution.

In 2004, **Serbia** established the Environmental Protection Agency within the Ministry of Environmental Protection and Spatial Planning, with the task of developing, harmonising and managing the National Environmental Information System, gathering, consolidating and processing environmental data, as well as drafting reports on the environmental status and implementation of the environmental protection policy. In 2008, Serbia adopted a National Sustainable Development Strategy which is structured around three pillars: knowledge-based sustainability, socio-economic conditions and environment and natural resources. To complement this general strategy several specific action programmes have been adopted. In addition, planning and management of environment protection is secured and provided by implementation of the National Environment Protection Programme, which contains short-term (2010-2014) and long-term objectives (2015-2019), National Waste Management Strategy (2010) and National Strategy for Biodiversity (2011).

The strategic goals of the Republic of **Albania** in the field of the environment are defined in the Environmental Cross-cutting Strategy (ECS). Many of the policies and measures of this strategy are supported by programmes and actions set out in inter-ministerial strategies. The effective implementation of the strategy lies with a number of institutions, but often inter-institutional bodies have been created to ensure co-ordination.

In 2008, the **Austrian** Government adopted comprehensive standards for public participation and recommended their application throughout the federal administration. Although the standards are not yet at present applied comprehensively, NGOs claim their application in the preparation of plans, programmes or policies in the environmental field.

In the **Czech Republic**, the Strategic Framework for Sustainable Development for 2010-2030 identifies key issues devoted to sustainable development and presents measures to address them. Apart from this overarching strategy there are other strategies and plans of action on particular issues in place, e.g. on abating climate change impacts, biodiversity protection, main catchment areas and waste management. The central role in environmental governance at national level is performed by the Ministry of the Environment and its special environmental bodies such as the Czech Environmental Inspectorate. Other ministries and/or national bodies are also involved in environmental protection.

In **Poland**, a National Environmental Policy is adopted for a period of four years in accordance with the Environmental Protection Law. It defines in particular the environmental objectives and priorities, the levels of long-term goals, the type and timing of environmental actions as well as measures necessary to achieve the objectives, including legal and economic mechanisms and financial resources.

In 2007, **Spain** adopted a Sustainable Development Strategy which includes "a long-term perspective to aim towards a more coherent society in terms of the rational use of its resources, and more equitable and cohesive approach and more balanced in terms of land use". The state legislation usually includes co-ordination mechanisms and planning directives. At the institutional level, an inter-territorial conference on environment regularly gathers the state and regional authorities competent for the environment and the Advisory Committee on Environment in which NGOs and other civil society organisations participate, to provide advice to the Ministry of Environment.

In **Switzerland**, plans of action are mainly contained in the national legislation processes. Furthermore, a National Biodiversity Strategy is under evaluation.

2. Establishing control over potentially harmful environmental activities

In **Belgium**, the authorisation of specific activities comes primarily within the remit of the regions. Nevertheless, the federal authority remains responsible for authorising the operation of nuclear activities as well as for authorising activities in marine areas that come under Belgian jurisdiction (North Sea).

In the **Slovak Republic**, the Constitution provides explicitly that the state shall care for economical exploitation of natural resources, ecological balance and effective environmental policy. It shall secure protection of determined sorts of wild plants and wild animals (Article 44).

In **Serbia**, the Law on Environmental Protection establishes manifold instruments to exercise various degrees of control over public and private activities which have an impact on the environment. It contains regulatory and other instruments such as permit regime, user and pollution fees and economic incentives. The law also contains an elaborated sanctioning regime for violators of environmental legislation, even criminal penalties are possible. This law implements the Seveso II Directive, which refers to harmful activities. In addition, three by-laws were passed based on the directive. Competence for law enforcement in the field of environmental protection is divided between: republic environmental protection inspections, provincial environmental protection, local environmental protection inspections.

In **Austria**, besides bans of massive damage to the environment and codes of conduct, permits issued by public authorities are prevailing, which means that activities (mostly economic) are subject to control exerted or permits granted by administrative authorities. Moreover, the Environmental Control Act provides that the Federal Minister responsible for the environment shall submit a written report on the state of implementation of environmental control to the Parliament every three years.

The **Bulgarian** Constitution states that subsurface resources (national roads, forests, beaches, water, etc.) constitute exclusive state property and that the state exercises the sovereign rights to the continental shelf and the maritime spaces (Article 18). The land as a basic national resource shall receive special protection by the state and the society (Article 21). The Environmental Protection Act ensures that anyone who culpably inflicts pollution or environmental damage on another shall be liable to indemnify the aggrieved party (Article 170).

In the **Czech Republic**, control over potentially harmful environmental activities is implemented through granting permissions and supervision of how these are implemented. A system of response measures provides for fines (penalties) and environmental liability. Institutionally the major burden is imposed on national and local authorities. Administrative and criminal courts are also considered part of this protection system as their role is not limited only to determining sanctions.

Similarly, in **Cyprus** environmental permits are issued to industrial and other plants by the Ministry of Labour to regulate air emissions, and by the Ministry of Agriculture regulating industrial waste, dangerous substances, water and soil pollution. The control of industrial pollution is achieved by the licensing of industrial installations and the systematic monitoring of their operation with on-site inspections so that the licensing standards and conditions are met and complied with. If need be, court orders may be obtained. Breach of environmental laws and violations of the conditions of a licence or permit give rise to criminal liability or civil liability for nuisance as well as for negligence for any damage sustained to person or property.

In **Germany**, various environmental laws provide that certain environmentally relevant activities may be commenced only after authorisation by the public authorities. Authorisation conditions aimed at protecting the environment are determined by statute, which are then reviewed by the public authorities in an authorisation procedure. To ensure compliance with obligations, sanctions are imposed for violations.

The Environmental Protection Law of **Poland** provides for a number of legal instruments aimed at establishing control over activities potentially harmful to the environment. For example, a permit issued by the competent authority is required for the operation of systems releasing gases or dust into the air, discharging sewage to water or soil and generating waste (Article 180). Another solution is the establishment of the National Pollutant Release and Transfer Register used to collect data on exceeding the applicable threshold values for releases and transfers of pollutants, and transfers of waste (Article 236a). Furthermore, the release of gases or dust into the air, the discharge of sewage to water or soil, water consumption and waste storage are subject to a charge for using the environment (Article 273). The Act also governs the issue of responsibility in environmental protection. An important role is also played by the Act on Preventing and Remedying Environmental Damage establishing a mechanism of accountability of entities using the environment for the imminent threat of damage to the environment and environmental damage. The Act on Inspection for Environmental Protection governs the performance of inspection by the Inspection of Environmental Protection, establishes the National Environmental Monitoring including information on the environment and its protection, and also refers to the execution of tasks in the event of environmental damage and major accidents.

Certain natural resources in **Spain** are considered public domain (territorial sea, beaches, rivers or certain forest). Its public use and the temporary exclusive use by concession are controlled in order to ensure its integrity and its preservation. In general, the establishment of environmental permits are used which allows the public administration to supervise that the private activity is developed in accordance with the requirements of the relevant environmental legislation (wastes, waste and chemicals, emissions of pollutants, etc.). In other cases, a prior communication or a responsible declaration must be presented to the public administration before the beginning of the activity, subjected to *ex post* supervision by the public authorities. Other preventive techniques are the certification or the regulation of the market of pollutions fees (CO_2). The Spanish law also establishes a system of sanctions, including criminal and administrative, and civil liability for causing environmental damage. For the enforcement of this legislation specialised units exist in the law enforcement agencies and in the Public Prosecutor Office.

In **Sweden**, environmental inspection and enforcement, referred to as "supervision" in the Environmental Code, are carried out by authorities at regional and local level and sometimes at national level. They are integrated in a single carefully balanced inspection and enforcement plan of each responsible authority in order to enable priority planning. To improve inspection efficiency the immediate enforcement authorities should regularly follow up and evaluate their planning and implementation. The Swedish Environmental Protection Agency has issued general guidelines for inspection planning. The Environmental Code also contains provisions on supervision and sanctions. The main enforcement instrument is administrative orders which can be combined with an administrative fine. The Code also includes environmental sanction charges and criminal penalties.

In **Switzerland** control over potentially harmful environmental activities is provided by the competent authorities either at the federal or at the cantonal level.

3. Requiring environmental impact assessments (EIAs)

By **Belgian** law the state is required to carry out substantial EIAs to guarantee its effective control over potentially harmful activities. For example, Article 28 of the Law of 20.01.1999 states that "any activity in marine areas that is subject to a permit or authorisation, [...] is subject to an environmental impact assessment by the competent authority appointed to this task by the Minister, both before and after granting the permit or authorisation. The EIA is designed to assess the effects of the activities on the marine environment."

The Nature Diversity Act of **Norway** also contains the requirement to undertake EIA to strike a fair balance between the various conflicting interests. Another very detailed example describing the requirements of an EIA is the **Hungarian** Act LIII of 1995.

According to the **Estonian** Act on Environmental Impact Assessment and Environmental Management System, the explicit goal of the EIA is to prevent and reduce potential environmental damage (Paragraph 2). The Act makes EIAs mandatory in cases where potentially a significant environmental impact could occur or where designated environmental protection sites (Natura 2000 sites) are impacted (paragraph 3). The Act defines environmental impact rather broadly as any direct or indirect effects of activities on human health and well-being, the environment, cultural heritage or property (paragraph 4). Moreover, it has defined that any irreversible change to the environment is considered "significant" (paragraph 5). In addition, the Act contains an extensive list of activities from mining to waste management or public infrastructure project which always require an EIA (paragraph 6). The Estonian Act also contains a section on "transboundary EIAs" (paragraph 30).

In **Austria**, EIAs are *inter alia* governed by the Impact Assessment Act. An EIA is mandatory for projects of the type included in Annex 1 of the Act and which meets certain threshold values or certain criteria specified for each type of project (e.g. production capacity, area of land used). The EIA as now practiced in Austria is a clear quality improvement over previous project licensing instruments, and is thus an important step towards precautionary and integrative environmental protection. It also serves as a planning instrument and a basis for decision-making. Moreover it gives environmental concerns the same degree of attention as any other and makes the project approval procedure more transparent and explicit by involving the public.

Also in **Poland**, the EIA is one of the basic legal instruments of environmental protection, considered the best expression of the principles of prevention and precaution in the investment process. The "Act on Access to Information about the Environment and its Protection, Public Participation in Environmental Protection and Environmental Impact Assessments" makes EIA a mandatory part of the decision-making process aiming at issuing a permit for the implementation of the proposed project, also serving as an auxiliary instrument for ensuring equal treatment of environmental aspects with social and economic issues. In Poland an important role is also played by the EU's instrument for organisations (enterprises and various institutions) - Eco-Management and Audit Scheme - which on a voluntary basis assesses the impact on the environment, in particular of small and medium enterprises and institutions whose individual effects may be relatively small - and therefore not subject to regular supervision by the environmental inspection services - but the sum of their impacts can be a significant burden to the environment.

The **Albanian** Law "On environmental protection" requires that activities with environmental impacts undergo an EIA process before implementation. Detailed EIA procedures are set forth in the Law "On the evaluation of environmental impact" (Chapter III). The activities are classified into two groups: Annex 1 applies to activities that require an in-depth EIA process, while Annex 2 lists the activities that need a summarised process of EIA. With a view to assessing possible adverse impacts on the environment, the law also foresees a review of applications for development. The Law "On the protection of the environment from transboundary effects" describes the procedure to follow for EIAs in a transboundary context.

The **Bulgarian** legislation regulates the issue of EIA in the Environmental Protection Act where it is stated that "An environmental assessment and an environmental impact assessment shall be performed in respect of plans, programmes and investment proposals for construction, activities and technologies, as well as amendments or extensions thereof, the implementation whereof entails the risk of significant impact on the environment..." (Article 81 (1)).

In the **Czech Republic**, certain activities and projects specified in the Act on Environmental Impact Assessment, which could have impact on public health and the environment, are subject to EIA. Impact assessment is required also for certain plans and programmes which may have effects on the environment. The Act implements relevant EU legislation and takes into account also international commitments of the Czech Republic under the Convention on Environmental Impact Assessment in a Transboundary Context (Espoo Convention).

In **Cyprus**, EIAs are required to be carried out under specific laws in relation to proposed private and public development projects in order to assess the possible effects of potentially harmful activities on, *inter alia*, human health, green areas, forests, water, property, and the environment generally. An Environmental Impact Assessment Committee was set up in 2001 to advise on environmental issues.

In **Serbia,** according to the Law on Environmental Impact Assessment construction projects may not commence without the prior completion of the impact assessment procedure. The EIA Study must be approved by the competent authority. This Law regulates the impact assessment procedure for projects that may have significant effects on the environment, the contents of the EIA Study, the participation of authorities and organisations concerned as well as the public, the transboundary exchange of information for projects that may have significant impact on the environment of another state, the supervision and other issues of relevance to the impact assessment. The participation of the public in all phases of an environment impact assessment is guaranteed through national legislation.

Under the **Spanish** Environmental Projects Assessments Law, EIA is a prerequisite before issuing a permit in the case of potentially harmful activities and infrastructure works. Besides, other legislation also provides EIAs of a preventive character for certain activities that could produce an important alteration of the public maritime and terrestrial domain (Coastal Area Law) or into the continental waters (Water Law).

According to the **Swedish** Environmental Code an EIA must be submitted together with a permit application. The purpose is to describe the direct and indirect impact of the planned activity. It must include a site description of the plant or activity as well as descriptions of the technology that will be used. Different alternatives for both these aspects are compulsory. The EIA must also describe the impact on people, animals, plants, land, water, air, climate, landscape and the cultural environment. Furthermore, it should describe impacts on the management of land, water and the physical environment in general, as well as on the management of materials, raw materials and energy.

Also **Switzerland** has enacted the obligation of performing an EIA for installations which are likely to cause extensive environmental contaminations (Article 10a ff. of the Environment Protection Act).

4. Securing public participation and access to information

In **Belgium** there is a general right of access to public documents, i.e. those stemming from public authorities, enshrined in Article 32 of the Constitution. Moreover, the specific "Law on public access to environmental information" has been established to implement the procedural rights guaranteed in the Aarhus Convention and EC directives. Additionally, Belgium has enacted the "Law on the assessment of the effects of certain plans and programmes on the environment and public participation in the elaboration of the plans and programmes relating to the environment". At the regional level several acts have been passed guaranteeing comparable rights.

The Environmental Information Act of **Norway** builds upon the obligations under the Aarhus Convention. It aims at facilitating public access to environmental information, in particular to the conclusions of environmental studies. According to the Act, administrative agencies are under duty to hold general environmental information relevant to their areas of responsibility and functions available and to make this information accessible to the public. Likewise "private undertakings", including commercial enterprises and other organised activities, are under a similar obligation to collect and provide information about factors relating to their activities which may have an appreciable effect on the environment. Any person is entitled to request such information.

Bulgaria has enshrined the right of access to information in its Environmental Protection Act. Article 17 explicitly mentions that it is not necessary for the information requesting party to prove a concrete interest, i.e. personal interest, to receive information.

The Environment Impact Assessment and Environmental Management System Act of **Estonia** also contains provisions on public information. For example, it requires public authorities to publish any conclusions of EIA (paragraph 16).

Like in Belgium, the right of access to information is in general guaranteed in the **Polish** Constitution (Article 74, paragraph 3). Poland has moreover implemented the Aarhus Convention and EU law through its "Act on access to information about the environment and its protection and public participation in environment protection and on the assessment of impact on the environment". The Act prescribes, *inter alia*, that individuals do not have to demonstrate a legal or factual interest. The Act also provides for public participation in projects with environmental impacts. To facilitate access to information Poland has established the Centre for Environmental Information. Emphasis has also been placed on making environmental information easily accessible by using online registers.

In the **Slovak Republic**, the Constitution guarantees the right of everyone to have full and timely information about the state of the environment and the causes and consequences of its condition (Article 45).

The same is the case for the **Serbian** Constitution (Article 74). The access to information of public importance is regulated mainly by the Law on Environmental Protection (Articles 78–82) and the Law on

Free Access to Information of Public Importance. Procedures for public participation have been developed by a series of recent laws: the Law on Environmental Protection, the Law on EIA, Law on Strategic Environmental Assessments (SEA) and the Law on the Internal Plant Protection Convention (IPPC).

Slovenia has enacted the Act on Access to Information of Public Character, which is not specific to the environment. Similar to Poland, Slovenia has made available online draft regulations and those in force, international agreements and other important documents to ensure maximum openness and transparency of its decision-making and legislative processes.

In **Albania**, the Framework Law "On Environmental Protection" sets out detailed rules on public participation in decision-making on environmental protection. It also guarantees the rights of individuals and environmental and professional NGOs to be informed and have access to environmental data. Additionally, as a Party to the Espoo Convention, Albania has adopted legislation which foresees the right of the public from neighbouring countries to participate in activities with a transborder impact.

In **Austria**, the term "environmental information" used in the Environmental Information Act is broadly phrased so that any kind of information on the state of the environment, factors, measures or activities (possibly) having an impact on the environment or conducive to the protection of the environment can be collected. The claim to environmental information is deemed an *actio popularis*. As it is not always easy for citizens to identify the body obliged to provide information, the Act provides for a respective duty to forward/refer the request for environmental information to the competent authorities.

Before granting permits or licences under certain laws, public authorities in **Cyprus** are required to obtain the views of any persons interested or who may be affected by the proposed plan or development and of local government boards and municipalities and to give such views due consideration.

In the **Czech Republic**, the Act on Administrative Procedure sets general principles for decision-making procedures within the public administration, including general rules for participation in the procedures. The person considered participant in the procedure is the one whose rights or obligations could be affected directly by the decision as well as everyone indicated as a participant under a special law (paragraph 27). In this context public participation in the decision-making process related to environmental issues is provided for by various special environmental acts.

In **Spain**, the Act 27/2006 guarantees access to environmental information and the diffusion and availability of environmental information to the public. This right is guaranteed without any obligation to declare a certain interest. The right to public participation on environmental matters can be exercised through certain administrative organs (the Advisory Council on Environment, the National Council for Climate Change, the Council for the Natural Heritage and Biodiversity, the National Council of Water, etc.). In addition, direct participation (in person or by representative associations) is possible in most administrative procedures and in the elaboration of procedure, plans or programmes on environmental matters.

Sweden has a long tradition of public participation in environmental decision-making, as well as of openness and transparency, or insight, in the activities of public authorities. For almost 40 years there has been an environmental permit procedure for industrial activities and other major installations with an environmental impact. Under the rules in the Environmental Code, anyone who intends to conduct an activity that requires a permit or a decision on permissibility has to consult with the country administrative board, the supervisory authority, and individuals who are likely to be particularly affected. The corresponding process is also guaranteed in transboundary contexts.

Under the principle of public access to official documents everyone in Sweden is entitled to examine the content of the information held by public authorities. This is even guaranteed in the Constitution (Chapter 2 of Act on Freedom of the Press).

Switzerland grants general access to information for public documents by its Freedom of Information Act. Moreover, Switzerland is in the process of acceding to the Aarhus Convention.

5. Making environmental rights judiciable and the environment a public concern

In **Belgium** not only individuals but also NGOs have various possibilities of obtaining access to justice through both judicial and administrative procedures. Generally, to have a standing in the Belgian Courts the applicant needs to prove that he or she has an interest in his or her claim. This has been interpreted by the Belgian

Supreme Court as to require the violation of one's own subjective rights. However, in response to this jurisprudence the Law of 12.01.1993 establishes the possibility for injunctive relieves to secure a general interest such as a manifest violation of legislative or regulatory provision on environmental protection or the serious risk of such a violation. This possibility has specifically been designed with environmental organisations in mind. The procedure is only open to national environmental non-lucrative organisations that have existed for at least three years. Moreover, NGOs and the public can turn to the Council of State to voice their complaints. In addition, the Law of 5.8.06 has created a Federal Appeal Committee for access to environmental information. Comparable procedures have been set up at the regional level as well.

Similar to Belgium, NGOs in **Switzerland that are** dedicated to environmental issues for at least ten years are entitled to access justice claiming a violation of the environmental legislation. Additionally, Article 6 of the Environment Protection Act states that authorities and individuals can seek and obtain advice on how to reduce environmental pollution from environmental protection agencies.

The **Hungarian** Act on the General Rules of Environmental Protection provides that natural and legal persons and unincorporated entities are entitled to participate in non-regulatory procedures concerning the environment. In particular, everyone has the right to call the attention of the user of the environment and the authorities to the fact that the environment is being endangered, damaged or polluted. It also allows environmental NGOs to be a party in proceedings concerning environmental protection. The Act, in addition, contains the idea of *actio popularis* stating that "in the event the environment is being endangered, damaged or polluted, organisations are entitled to intervene in the interest of protecting the environment" which includes filing a lawsuit against the user of the environment (Section 99). Additionally, Hungary has established the Office of the Environment Ombudsman to facilitate public complaints in environmental matters.

Similarly, in **Slovenia** the possibility exists of an *actio popularis* to protect the environment. According to Article 14 of the Environment Protection Act, in order to exercise their right to a healthy living environment, citizens may, as individuals or through societies, file a request with the judiciary. Ultimately, by such a request citizens can oblige a person responsible for an activity affecting the environment, to cease such an activity if it causes or would cause an excessive environmental burden or presents a direct threat to human life or health. Moreover, this can lead to the prohibition of starting an activity which affects the environment if there is a strong probability that the activity will present such a threat. In addition, the Supreme Court has recognised the right to a healthy living environment as one of the personal rights for whose violation compensation and just satisfaction can be claimed.

Poland's "Act on the access to information about the environment and its protection and public participation in environment protection and on the assessment of impact on the environment" also ensures public access to justice on environment related matters. This involves, for example, the right of environmental organisations to take part in proceedings with the right of being a party and to appeal against a decision and file a complaint with the administrative court, also in cases when the organisation did not take part in the given proceedings requiring public participation.

The **Albanian** Law on Environmental Protection ensures that any individual or organisation may start legal proceedings in a court regarding environment related matters (Article 81). More specifically, in case of a threat to, or damage or pollution of the environment, individuals, the general public and non-profit organisations are entitled to the right to make an administrative complaint, and to start legal proceedings in a court of law. However, according to the Code of Administrative Procedures, the complainant needs to have exhausted all the administrative procedures before going to court (Article 137.3). This means that the complainant should first seek an administrative review from the relevant public authority and then appeal that decision at a higher body, before going to court. Environment related reviews or appeals may also be lodged with the Ombudsman.

The **Austrian** legal system provides several possibilities for enforcing environmental matters. In general, according to the Civil Code, anybody who is or fears of being endangered by pollution is entitled to file a lawsuit against the polluter and to seek an injunction. This right to preventive action against pollution detrimental to health has been expressly acknowledged by courts as an integral, innate right of every natural person (Section 16), neither requiring participation in administrative proceedings nor ownership of private property in the proximity of the polluter. In addition, private entities in violation of environmental laws may be sued by competitors and special interest groups, since producing goods in violation of such laws is regarded by courts to be unfair competition. Furthermore, neighbours hold the individual right to prohibit emissions exceeding a certain level (Section 364 et seq). In this context, direct or indirect emissions having an effect from one property to another (e.g. waste water, smell, noise, light and radiation) are deemed as impairments. In addition, special laws provide for claims for damages related to the environment. Most of Austrian provisions on the protection of the environment are, however, of an administrative nature. The application and administration of such laws is subject to an effective appeal mechanism and can finally be challenged at the Administrative Court and/or the Constitutional Court. In addition, at regional level Environmental Advocacy Offices i.e. Ombudsmen for the environment have been set up who, in the position as parties, are authorised to lodge complaints with the Administrative Court with regard to compliance with legal provisions which are relevant for the environment. Furthermore, the Federal Environmental Liability Act provides for an environmental complaint, if the public authority fails to take action in the event of environmental damage (to water and soil, provided that human health is affected).

In **Cyprus,** natural or legal persons have a right under Article 146 of the Constitution to file a recourse to the Supreme Court against "any decision, act or omission of any organ, authority or person exercising any executive or administrative authority" if certain conditions are met. The complainant must have an "existing legitimate interest" which is adversely and directly affected. Class actions are not therefore available, as the interest required must be personal to the complainant. Nonetheless the Supreme Court's jurisprudence has extended the definition of "existing legitimate interest" to include local government boards and municipalities, but only in cases where the local natural environment is of a direct interest to or is the responsibility of the complainant community as a whole.

In the **Czech Republic,** the right to appeal against a decision issued by an administrative authority is guaranteed. The appeal procedure is governed by the Act on Administrative Procedure and special environmental laws. Access to judicial protection in case of public environmental concern is regulated only through general provisions of the Act on Judicial Administrative Procedure. In this context a special legal status in order to protect public interests is given by the law to the Attorney General and also to a person to whom a special law, or an international treaty which is a part of the Czech legal order, explicitly commits this authorisation (§ 66).

In **Spain,** citizens, NGOs or any other entity who exercise the right of access to information may challenge before the administrative authorities any decision refusing the information requested and, if the denial decision is ratified, before the judicial authorities. The Act 27/2006 allows a request of the access to information from natural or legal persons acting on behalf or by delegation of any public authority. The decision adopted by the Public Administration is mandatory to the private person and is enforceable by coercive fines. In addition, on environmental matters, NGOs and other non-profit entities (under certain conditions) may exercise before the courts an *actio popularis* against any administrative decision, or the failure to adopt it, violating the environmental rules.

In **Sweden**, the right to appeal a decision concerning the release of an official document is set out in both the Freedom of the Press Act (Chapter 2, Article 15) and the Public Access to Information and Secrecy Act (Chapter 6, Section 7). The right to a determination by a court of law of the substantive and formal validity of decisions, etc., is provided for in different parts of Swedish legislation. This is particularly the case for permit decisions taken under the rules of the Environmental Code as well as permit decisions taken by the government in accordance with the Act on Judicial Review of Certain Government Decisions. Under the latter Act, environmental NGOs also have an explicit right to apply for judicial review of permit decisions by the government that are covered by article 9, paragraph 2, of the Aarhus Convention. In the case of environmental decisions issued under the Planning and Building Act, new rules in that Act also give environmental NGOs the right to appeal such decisions. In accordance with the Environmental Code as well as a number of other specialised acts, decisions may be appealed by a person who is affected by the decision if it has gone against him or her, by environmental NGOs, and by non-profit organisations that have safeguarded the interests of nature conservation or environmental protection as their main aim, that have at least 100 members or prove by other means that they have the support of the public, and that have conducted activities in Sweden for at least three years.

To ensure that authorities handle their business correctly, the actions and omissions of the public authorities in Sweden are examined by the Parliamentary Ombudsmen and the Chancellor of Justice. The public, including environmental NGOs, are always able to report infringements of various environmental regulations to supervisory authorities, and the public can also take direct contact with the Parliamentary Ombudsmen, who examine complaints concerning deficiencies and omissions in the exercise of public authority.

In **Serbia**, the Law on Environmental Protection, on EIA, on Strategic Environmental Assessment (SEA) and on the International Plant Protection Convention (IPPC) enable individuals and organisations (including non-governmental organisations) to file administrative complaints and access courts in environmental matters. This environmental legislation envisages that individuals or organisations concerned with environmental development can initiate a decision review procedure before the responsibility authorities or a court. Those who do not have legal personality (e.g. state bodies, community organisations) can participate in the review process if they have a legal interest in the proceedings or hold specific rights and obligations (Article 40 paragraph 1 and 2 of the Law on General Administrative Procedure). The plaintiff in administrative disputes may be a natural, legal or other person, if considers to be deprived of certain right or interest provided by law by administrative act (Article 11 of the Law on Administrative Disputes).

In addition, each natural or legal person, – domestic or foreign – who believes that his/her rights were breached by the action or a failure to act by a public authority is entitled to lodge a complaint with the Ombudsman. The Ombudsman will refer the applicant to the relevant authorities to initiate legal proceedings, if all legal remedies have been exhausted (Article 25 of the Law on the Ombudsman).

Anybody can demand from another person to remove sources of hazard of serious damage to him/her personally or to the general public (indefinite number of people). He can also demand the cessation of activity inducing harassment or damage hazard if the harassment or damage can not be prevented by appropriate measures (Article 156 paragraph 1 of the Law on Obligatory Relations). Article 54 of the Criminal Procedure Code prescribes that the proposal for criminal prosecution should be lodged to the competent public prosecutor, and the proposal for private prosecution to the competent court.

Appendix V: Useful websites

Council of Europe	
Council of Europe's website on climate change	www.coe.int/lportal/web/coe-portal/what-we-do/culture-and-nature/climate-change
European Court of Human Rights	www.echr.coe.int
Hudoc – the online database of the Court's case-law	http://hudoc.echr.coe.int
European Court of Human Rights Case Fact Sheets – continually updated case summaries on various environmental issues	www.echr.coe.int/echr/en/header/press/information+sheets/factsheets
European Social Charter	www.coe.int/T/E/Human_Rights/Esc
See also: European Social Charter – Collected Texts, 6th edition (30 June 2008):	www.coe.int/t/dghl/monitoring/socialcharter/Presentation/ESCCollectedTexts_en.pdf

Parliamentary Assembly Committee on the Environment, Agriculture and Local and Regional Affairs	http://assembly.coe.int/Main.asp?link=/committee/CULT/index_E.htm

European Union

European Union's portal to EU law	http://eur-lex.europa.eu/en/index.htm
European Commission environment porta	http://ec.europa.eu/environment/index_en.htm
European Environment Agency (EEA	www.eea.europa.eu The EEA's task is to provide sound, independent information on the environment for those involved in developing, adopting, implementing and evaluating environmental policy, but also for the general public. Currently, the EEA has 32 member countries.
EU Network for the Implementation and Enforcement of Environmental Law	http://impel.eu IMPEL is a network of environmental authorities in Europe. The network is committed to contributing to a more effective application of EU Environmental law.

United Nations

UN Economic Commission for Europe: activities related to the environment	www.unece.org/env/welcome.html
Aarhus Convention's official website	www.unece.org/env/pp/welcome.html This website provides the text of the Convention, status of ratification and publications, as well as a number of other documents, guides and information tools.
Convention on Environmental Impact Assessment in a Transboundary Context (Espoo Convention)	www.unece.org/env/eia/welcome.html

United Nations Environment Programme (UNEP)	www.unep.org/ www.unep.org/resources/gov/keydocuments.asp High Level Expert Meeting on the New Future of Human Rights and Environment: Moving the Global Agenda Forward and related materials www.unep.org/environmentalgovernance/Events/ HumanRightsandEnvironment/tabid/2046/language/ en-US/Default.aspx
World Trade Organisation	
World Trade Organisation Portal on Trade and Environment	www.wto.org/english/tratop_e/envir_e/envir_e.htm The portal also contains explanations of the WTO legal framework for the protection of the environment including which restrictions are permissible.
Other informative websites	
European Environmental Law (EEL)	www.eel.nl This site contains the text of relevant case-law, national legislation and other documents related to European environmental law. It also gathers complete dossiers on specific issues.
ECOLEX	www.ecolex.org ECOLEX is a comprehensive database, operated jointly by the IUCN (the World Conservation Union), UNEP and FAO (the Food and Agriculture Organization of the UN). It gives basic information about relevant treaties, national legislation or court decisions and provides technical as well as literature references.
REC (the Regional Environmental Center for central and eastern Europe)	www.rec.org Established in 1990, the REC provides assistance to resolve environmental problems in central and eastern Europe. The REC's website contains valuable information on the developments which are taking place in central and eastern Europe. It also provides an extended bibliography and study cases on the Aarhus Convention, public access to information, public participation and access to justice.

IEEP (Institute for European Environmental Policy)	www.ieep.eu The IEEP website is a comprehensive list of links connected to environmental law and policy regarding the European Union from an independent, non-profit organisation.
Global Network for the Study of Human Rights and the Environment	http://gnhre.uwe.ac.uk/RenderPages/ RenderHomePage.aspx

Appendix VI: Further reading

The literature listed in this appendix provides some additional information on the current state and interpretation of contemporary international environmental law, the European Convention on Human Rights and the European Social Charter with reference to the environment. The list is thought to complement the objective summary of the case-law of the Court and the Committee through academic analysis.

Alston, Philip/Goodman, Ryan and Steiner, Henry J.

International Human Rights in Context. Law, Politics, Morals, Oxford University Press, 3rd edition (2007)

Alfredsson, Gudmundur

Human Rights and the Environment in: Leary, David and Pisupati, Balakrishna (Eds.): The Future Of International Environmental Law, United Nations University Press (2010), p. 127

Anton, Donald K. and Shelton Dinah L.

The Environment and Human Rights, Cambridge University Press (2011)

Birnie Patricia/ Boyle, Alan and Redgwell, Catherine

International Law and the Environment, Oxford University Press, 3rd edition (2009)

Boyle, Alan

Human Rights and the Environment: A Reassessment, UNEP Paper 2010, available at: www.unep.org/environmentalgovernance/LinkClick.aspx?fileticket=GccCLN-brmg%3D&tabid=2046&language=en-US

Bodansky, Daniel/Brunnee, Jutta/Hey, Ellen

The Oxford Handbook of International Environmental Law, Oxford University Press (2008)

Déjeant-Pons, Maguelonne and Pallemaerts, Marc (Eds.)

Human Rights and the Environment, Compendium of instruments and other international texts on individual and collective rights relating to the environment in the international and European framework, Council of Europe Publishing (2002)

Francioni, Francesco

International Human Rights in an Environmental Horizon, European Journal of International Law, Vol. 21 p. 41 (February 2010)

Fitzmaurice, Malgosia

The European Court of Human Rights, Environmental Damage and the Applicability of Article 8 of the European Convention on Human Rights and Fundamental Freedoms, Environmental Law Review, Vol. 13 Issue 2 p. 107 (May 2011)

García San José, Daniel

Environmental Protection and the European Convention on Human Rights, Human Rights Files, No. 21, Council of Europe Publishing (2005) (also in French)

Glazebrook, Susan

Human Rights and the Environment, Victoria University of Wellington Law Review, Vol. 40 No. 1 p. 293 (June 2009)

Gouritin, Armelle

Potential liability of European States under the ECHR for failure to take appropriate measures with a view to adaptation to climate change, Ius Commune Workshop Environmental Law, 27 November 2009, published in: Faure, Michael and Peeters, Marjan (Eds.): Climate Change Liability, Edward Elgar Publishing, p. 134 (2011)

Loucaides, Loukis

Environmental Protection through the Jurisprudence of the European Convention on Human Rights, British Yearbook of International Law, Vol. 75 p. 249 (2005)

MacDonald, Karen E.

A Right to a Healthful Environment -Humans and Habitats: Re-thinking Rights in an Age of Climate Change, European Energy and Environmental Law Review, Vol. 17 Issue 4, p. 213 (August 2008)

Pallemaerts, Marc

Human Rights and Sustainable Spatial Development, in: Proceedings of the International CEMAT Symposium on "The Spatial Dimension of Human Rights: For a New Culture of the Territory", Yerevan, Armenia, 13-14 October 2008, European Spatial Planning and Landscape Series No. 91, Council of Europe Publishing p. 45, (2009), available at: www.coe.int/t/dg4/cultureheritage/heritage/Landscape/Publications/ATEP-91Assemble_bil.pdf

Pallemaerts, Marc

A Human Rights Perspective on Current Environmental Issues and Their Management: Evolving International Legal and Political Discourse on the Human Environment, the Individual and the State, Human Rights & International Legal Discourse, Vol. 2 p. 149 (2008)

Pedersen, Ole W.

The ties that bind: the Environment, the European Convention on Human Rights and the Rule of Law, European Public Law, Vol. 16 Issue 4, p. 571 (December 2010)

Pedersen, Ole W.

European Environmental Human Rights and Environmental Rights: A Long Time Coming?, Georgetown International Environmental Law Review, Vol. 21 p. 73 (2008)

Schall, Christian

Public Interest Litigation Concerning Environmental Matters Before Human Rights Courts: A Promising Future Concept?, Journal of Environmental Law, Vol. 20. p. 417 (2008)

Shelton, Dinah L.

Developing Substantive Environmental Rights, Journal of Human Rights and the Environment, Vol. 1 no. 1. p. 89 (2010).

Shelton, Dinah L.

International Decision: Tâtar v. Romania, American Journal of International Law, Vol. 104 p. 247 (2010)

Trilsch, Mirja

European Committee of Social Rights: The right to a healthy environment,
International Journal of Constitutional Law, Vol. 7 p. 529 (July 2009)

Appendix VII: Keyword index

A, B, C

D

E

F

G, H, I, J, K, L

M, N, O

no-harm principle 138, 141, 149

noise 46–47, 49, 52, 54, 57, 88, 105, 153

non-governmental organisation 24, 79, 100, 117, 131

nuclear
power plant 26–27, 98–99, 127, 151–152
weapon 36, 113–114, 133–134, 149

nuclear See radiation (nuclear)

Obligation to respect human rights (Article 1 ECHR)
exceptional circumstances allowing for the ECHRs extra-territorial application 113
jurisdiction primarily territorial 113
link to general environmental law 115, 149

obligation to respect human rights (Article 1 ECHR) 25

oil spillage 25, 107, 157

P

polluter pays principle 139, 141, 154

pollution 45–46, 96
air 26, 48, 59, 124–125, 149
attribution 48, 136, 139
cumulative effect 49
maritime 25, 107, 153–154, 157
soil 49, 59
water 49, 59, 96, 134

positive obligations 132, 138–139

possessions, peaceful enjoyment of 139

precautionary principle 50, 139, 141, 150, 155–156

prevention principle 140–141

prohibition of torture, inhuman and degrading treatment (Article 3) 8

proportionality 140

protection of property (Article 1 Protocol No. 1 ECHR) 20, 61
compensation 68–69, 71
control of the use of property 21, 62, 65
demolition of housing 66–69
expropriation 63, 68

land planning/building permits 65–68, 70, 98
link to Article 13 (right to an effective remedy) 105
link to Article 2 (right to life) 73
obligation to guarantee the peaceful enjoyment of possessions 21, 65, 71, 139
obligation to protect from environmental risk 72
obligation to provide for a complaints mechanism 23, 95, 106
positive obligation, scope of 21, 71, 73
possessions, definition 62, 72
restrictions to 21, 63–65, 67, 69–71, 140
scope of protection (ratione materiae) 21, 62, 72, 133

protest 77, 79, 100

provision of information principle 132

public authorities 31, 140

public house (pub) 52

public interest 52, 70, 140

public participation principle 140

R

Sales agents for publications of the Council of Europe
Agents de vente des publications du Conseil de l'Europe

BELGIUM/BELGIQUE
La Librairie Européenne -
The European Bookshop
Rue de l'Orme, 1
BE-1040 BRUXELLES
Tel.: +32 (0)2 231 04 35
Fax: +32 (0)2 735 08 60
E-mail: order@libeurop.be
http://www.libeurop.be

Jean De Lannoy/DL Services
Avenue du Roi 202 Koningslaan
BE-1190 BRUXELLES
Tel.: +32 (0)2 538 43 08
Fax: +32 (0)2 538 08 41
E-mail: jean.de.lannoy@dl-servi.com
http://www.jean-de-lannoy.be

BOSNIA AND HERZEGOVINA/
BOSNIE-HERZÉGOVINE
Robert's Plus d.o.o.
Marka Maruliça 2/V
BA-71000, SARAJEVO
Tel.: + 387 33 640 818
Fax: + 387 33 640 818
E-mail: robertsplus@bih.net.ba

CANADA
Renouf Publishing Co. Ltd.
1-5369 Canotek Road
CA-OTTAWA, Ontario K1J 9J3
Tel.: +1 613 745 2665
Fax: +1 613 745 7660
Toll-Free Tel.: (866) 767-6766
E-mail: order.dept@renoufbooks.com
http://www.renoufbooks.com

CROATIA/CROATIE
Robert's Plus d.o.o.
Marasoviçeva 67
HR-21000, SPLIT
Tel.: + 385 21 315 800, 801, 802, 803
Fax: + 385 21 315 804
E-mail: robertsplus@robertsplus.hr

CZECH REPUBLIC/
RÉPUBLIQUE TCHÈQUE
Suweco CZ, s.r.o.
Klecakova 347
CZ-180 21 PRAHA 9
Tel.: +420 2 424 59 204
Fax: +420 2 848 21 646
E-mail: import@suweco.cz
http://www.suweco.cz

DENMARK/DANEMARK
GAD
Vimmelskaftet 32
DK-1161 KØBENHAVN K
Tel.: +45 77 66 60 00
Fax: +45 77 66 60 01
E-mail: gad@gad.dk
http://www.gad.dk

FINLAND/FINLANDE
Akateeminen Kirjakauppa
PO Box 128
Keskuskatu 1
FI-00100 HELSINKI
Tel.: +358 (0)9 121 4430
Fax: +358 (0)9 121 4242
E-mail: akatilaus@akateeminen.com
http://www.akateeminen.com

FRANCE
La Documentation française
(diffusion/distribution France entière)
124, rue Henri Barbusse
FR-93308 AUBERVILLIERS CEDEX
Tél.: +33 (0)1 40 15 70 00
Fax: +33 (0)1 40 15 68 00
E-mail: commande@ladocumentationfrancaise.fr
http://www.ladocumentationfrancaise.fr

Librairie Kléber
1 rue des Francs Bourgeois
FR-67000 STRASBOURG
Tel.: +33 (0)3 88 15 78 88
Fax: +33 (0)3 88 15 78 80
E-mail: librairie-kleber@coe.int
http://www.librairie-kleber.com

GERMANY/ALLEMAGNE
AUSTRIA/AUTRICHE
UNO Verlag GmbH
August-Bebel-Allee 6
DE-53175 BONN
Tel.: +49 (0)228 94 90 20
Fax: +49 (0)228 94 90 222
E-mail: bestellung@uno-verlag.de
http://www.uno-verlag.de

GREECE/GRÈCE
Librairie Kauffmann s.a.
Stadiou 28
GR-105 64 ATHINAI
Tel.: +30 210 32 55 321
Fax.: +30 210 32 30 320
E-mail: ord@otenet.gr
http://www.kauffmann.gr

HUNGARY/HONGRIE
Euro Info Service
Pannónia u. 58.
PF. 1039
HU-1136 BUDAPEST
Tel.: +36 1 329 2170
Fax: +36 1 349 2053
E-mail: euroinfo@euroinfo.hu
http://www.euroinfo.hu

ITALY/ITALIE
Licosa SpA
Via Duca di Calabria, 1/1
IT-50125 FIRENZE
Tel.: +39 0556 483215
Fax: +39 0556 41257
E-mail: licosa@licosa.com
http://www.licosa.com

MEXICO/MEXIQUE
Mundi-Prensa México, S.A. De C.V.
Río Pánuco, 141 Delegacion Cuauhtémoc
MX-06500 MÉXICO, D.F.
Tel.: +52 (01)55 55 33 56 58
Fax: +52 (01)55 55 14 67 99
E-mail: mundiprensa@mundiprensa.com.mx
http://www.mundiprensa.com.mx

NETHERLANDS/PAYS-BAS
Roodveldt Import BV
Nieuwe Hemweg 50
NL-1013 CX AMSTERDAM
Tel.: + 31 20 622 8035
Fax.: + 31 20 625 5493
Website: www.publidis.org
Email: orders@publidis.org

NORWAY/NORVÈGE
Akademika
Postboks 84 Blindern
NO-0314 OSLO
Tel.: +47 2 218 8100
Fax: +47 2 218 8103
E-mail: support@akademika.no
http://www.akademika.no

POLAND/POLOGNE
Ars Polona JSC
25 Obroncow Street
PL-03-933 WARSZAWA
Tel.: +48 (0)22 509 86 00
Fax: +48 (0)22 509 86 10
E-mail: arspolona@arspolona.com.pl
http://www.arspolona.com.pl

PORTUGAL
Livraria Portugal
(Dias & Andrade, Lda.)
Rua do Carmo, 70
PT-1200-094 LISBOA
Tel.: +351 21 347 42 82 / 85
Fax: +351 21 347 02 64
E-mail: info@livrariaportugal.pt
http://www.livrariaportugal.pt

RUSSIAN FEDERATION/
FÉDÉRATION DE RUSSIE
Ves Mir
17b, Butlerova.ul.
RU-117342 MOSCOW
Tel.: +7 495 739 0971
Fax: +7 495 739 0971
E-mail: orders@vesmirbooks.ru
http://www.vesmirbooks.ru

SPAIN/ESPAGNE
Mundi-Prensa Libros, s.a.
Castelló, 37
ES-28001 MADRID
Tel.: +34 914 36 37 00
Fax: +34 915 75 39 98
E-mail: libreria@mundiprensa.es
http://www.mundiprensa.com

SWITZERLAND/SUISSE
Planetis Sàrl
16 chemin des Pins
CH-1273 ARZIER
Tel.: +41 22 366 51 77
Fax: +41 22 366 51 78
E-mail: info@planetis.ch

UNITED KINGDOM/ROYAUME-UNI
The Stationery Office Ltd
PO Box 29
GB-NORWICH NR3 1GN
Tel.: +44 (0)870 600 5522
Fax: +44 (0)870 600 5533
E-mail: book.enquiries@tso.co.uk
http://www.tsoshop.co.uk

UNITED STATES and CANADA/
ÉTATS-UNIS et CANADA
Manhattan Publishing Co
2036 Albany Post Road
USA-10520 CROTON ON HUDSON, NY
Tel.: +1 914 271 5194
Fax: +1 914 271 5886
E-mail: coe@manhattanpublishing.coe
http://www.manhattanpublishing.com

Council of Europe Publishing/Editions du Conseil de l'Europe
FR-67075 STRASBOURG Cedex
Tel.: +33 (0)3 88 41 25 81 – Fax: +33 (0)3 88 41 39 10 – E-mail: publishing@coe.int – Website: http://book.coe.int